Portraits Of Coastal Commerce

Portraits Of Coastal Commerce

Rayan Musk

Noble Publishing

Contents

INDEX	1
Introduction	3
Chapter 1	9
Chapter 2	25
Chapter 3	43
Chapter 4	57
Chapter 5	72
Chapter 6	87
Chapter 7	104
Chapter 8	120
Chapter 9	140

INDEX

Introduction

Chapter 1: Setting Sail
1.1 Introduction to coastal commerce and its historical significance
1.2 Overview of key coastal trading routes and their impact on global economies
1.3 The role of ports and coastal cities in facilitating trade and commerce

Chapter 2: The Maritime Marketplace
2.1 Exploration of diverse industries thriving in coastal regions
2.2 Successful coastal businesses and their impact on local economies
2.3 Analysis of how geographical factors influence the types of commerce in different coastal areas

Chapter 3: Tides of Innovation
3.1 Examination of technological advancements in coastal commerce
3.2 Impact of digitalization and automation on shipping, logistics, and port operations
3.3 Interviews with industry leaders on embracing innovation to stay competitive

Chapter 4: Environmental Challenges and Sustainable Solutions
4.1 Discussion on the environmental impact of coastal commerce
4.2 Businesses adopting sustainable practices
4.3 Exploration of green technologies in shipping and coastal industries

Chapter 5: Coastal Communities and Cultural Commerce
5.1 Spotlight on the unique cultures and communities shaped by coastal commerce

5.2 Exploration of local businesses, traditions, and customs influenced by maritime trade

5.3 Interviews with individuals who have made significant contributions to coastal economies

Chapter 6: Navigating Regulatory Waters

6.1 Overview of international maritime laws and regulations

6.2 Analysis of how regulatory frameworks impact coastal businesses

6.3 Companies adapting to and thriving within regulatory constraints

Chapter 7: Challenges on the Horizon

7.1 Examination of current challenges facing coastal commerce, such as climate change and geopolitical tensions

7.2 Interviews with experts on potential future challenges and their implications for coastal economies

7.3 Strategies for businesses to adapt and navigate uncertain waters

Chapter 8: Resilience in the Storm

8.1 Stories of coastal businesses overcoming adversity and economic downturns

8.2 Lessons learned from historical events that have shaped the resilience of coastal economies

8.3 Tips for businesses to build resilience and thrive in turbulent economic conditions

Chapter 9: Charting the Future

9.1 Exploration of emerging trends in coastal commerce

9.2 Interviews with futurists and industry experts on the future of maritime trade

9.3 Recommendations for businesses to prepare for and capitalize on future opportunities in coastal commerce

Introduction

The seaside scene, with its musical recurring pattern, has for quite some time been a material for the unpredictable dance of trade. Along the shores where land meets ocean, a rich embroidery of monetary exercises unfurls, uncovering the cooperative connection between human undertaking and the tremendous territory of the sea. From clamoring port urban communities to interesting fishing towns, the seaside zones demonstrate the veracity of the different essences of business, each recounting a novel story of exchange, industry, and the consistently changing tides of flourishing.

In the core of this sea theater, significant port urban areas stand as sentinels of worldwide network. Secured in history and powered by advancement, these center points of trade act as entryways to the world. One such city is Rotterdam, where the rambling port complex expands its arrive at like the fingers of an innovative monster. Here, titanic holder ships explore the waters, conveying with them the soul of global exchange. The complex movement of cranes and holders is a visual ensemble that highlights the effectiveness and size of present day oceanic trade.

However, past the loftiness of significant ports, the beach front scene is embellished with more modest harbors and straights, each adding to the financial mosaic in its own particular manner. Fishing towns like those along the tough banks of Newfoundland illustrate waterfront trade. Here, the murmur of apparatus is supplanted by the cadenced squeaking of wooden boats, and the fragrance of salted air blends with the smell of newly gotten fish. In these affectionate networks, ages have relied upon the abundance of the ocean, fashioning an immortal association among work and the steadily changing mind-sets of the sea.

The beach front business account reaches out past the actual trade of products. It winds around a story of social trade, where the back and forth movement of exchange carry with them a kaleidoscope of impacts. In noteworthy ports like Istanbul, the combination of East and West is obvious. The clamoring markets and twisted roads recount an account of exceptionally old shipping lanes that have formed the actual texture of the city. Silks from the East blend with flavors from the South, making a commercial center that is both a demonstration of variety and a living demonstration of the persevering through force of waterfront trade to connect far off shores.

As we dig further into the representations of waterfront trade, we experience the imperceptible strings that tight spot economies and countries. The oceanic shipping lanes, antiquated in beginning yet unendingly advancing, structure the courses of worldwide trade. From the antiquated Silk Street to the current delivery paths of the Suez Channel, these oceanic expressways have associated mainlands and worked with the trading of products, thoughts, and societies.

The essential significance of these courses couldn't possibly be more significant, as they act as conductors for the progression of merchandise that support economies and shape the predeterminations of countries.

In the shadow of these sea thruways, beach front urban communities have ascended as monetary forces to be reckoned with. Hong Kong, with its notable horizon set against the scenery of Victoria Harbor, remains as a demonstration of the groundbreaking power of waterfront business. When a modest fishing town, it has developed into a worldwide monetary center point, where the flows of exchange meet with the flows of capital. The horizon, interspersed by transcending high rises, reflects the goals of a city that has tackled the energy of the ocean to impel itself to monetary conspicuousness.

However, not all waterfront trade is estimated in the size of super urban communities and clamoring ports. Along the quiet shores of Kerala, India, conventional wooden boats known as "kettuvallams" quietly float through the mind boggling organization of backwaters. Weighed down with flavors and nearby produce, these vessels are the help of a district where business is well established in the practices of the land. The backwaters, when the sole space of neighborhood exchange, have now turned into a magnet for travelers looking for a brief look into the delicate speed of beach front trade entwined with the immortal magnificence of the scene.

In the domain of seaside trade, advancement has forever been the breeze in the sails of progress. The approach of containerization altered the delivery business, permitting merchandise to be shipped with extraordinary effectiveness. The normalization of delivery compartments smoothed out the stacking and dumping processes as well as worked with consistent multi-purpose transportation, interfacing the sea space with the tremendous hinterlands. The effect of this development is noticeable in ports around the world, where compartment terminals structure the foundation of current exchange.

Essentially, progressions in route innovation have changed the wellbeing and effectiveness of sea transportation. From the old astrolabe to the advanced GPS, the instruments of route have developed, decreasing the vulnerabilities of the vast ocean. Radar frameworks penetrate the obscurity, directing boats through mist loaded waters, while satellite correspondence guarantees that vessels stay associated with the worldwide organization even in the remotest stretches of the sea. These developments, conceived out of the mission for more secure and more solid ocean courses, have reshaped the shapes of waterfront business.

As we navigate the worldwide seascape, it becomes clear that beach front business isn't safe to the difficulties presented essentially. The wrath of tempests, the erratic impulses of sea flows, and the ghost of rising ocean levels cast a shadow over the monetary exercises that unfurl along the coast. In low-lying locales like the Netherlands, where a huge piece of the land lies underneath ocean level, imaginative designing arrangements have been conveyed to fight off the infringing waters.

The famous windmills, when images of agrarian life, presently stand as watchmen of a scene that is inseparably connected to the back and forth movement of both trade and the tides.

Even with natural difficulties, the idea of economical waterfront trade has acquired unmistakable quality. Seaside environments, delicate yet versatile, are imperative to the wellbeing of the planet. Mangroves, with their complicated root foundations, give a characteristic hindrance against seaside disintegration and act as nurseries for marine life. Endeavors to offset financial improvement with natural protection have prompted the development of eco-accommodating practices in seaside trade. Feasible fishing techniques, eco-the travel industry drives, and the reclamation of waterfront living spaces all add to a dream of business that blends with the sensitive equilibrium of nature.

The charm of seaside business reaches out past the domain of substantial merchandise, embracing the elusive domain of thoughts and social trade. In the old port city of Alexandria, the Incomparable Library remained as a guide of information, drawing researchers and scholars from across the well explored regions of the planet. The trading of thoughts that occurred inside its blessed lobbies rose above the limits of topography and established the groundwork for the scholarly embroidery of human progress. The reverberations of this heritage resound in current seaside urban communities, where colleges and examination establishments stand as advanced guides of scholarly trade.

As we explore the flows of time, the oceanic Silk Street of the past tracks down its contemporary partner in the advanced Silk Street of the present. The data expressway, spreading over the globe with fiber-optic links and satellite connections, has changed the idea of beach front business. Online business stages associate purchasers and dealers across landmasses, and advanced monetary forms navigate the virtual oceans of the web, reshaping the scene of global money. The limits among physical and virtual trade obscure, making a dynamic and interconnected worldwide commercial center.

Waterfront trade, be that as it may, isn't just an account of wins and progress. It is likewise a story set apart by the shadows of double-dealing and imbalance. The memorable ports where flavors and valuable merchandise once streamed have, now and again, been stained by the more obscure sections of mankind's set of experiences. The transoceanic slave exchange, filled by the interest for work in the ranches of the Americas, cast a long and difficult shadow over the historical backdrop of beach front trade. The eerie reverberations of this insensitive exchange advise us that the waters that convey thriving likewise give testimony regarding the scars of double-dealing.

In the contemporary time, the differences in the advantages of seaside trade are obvious on a worldwide scale. While a few beach front locales prosper as monetary forces to be reckoned with, others mope in neediness and disregard.

The idea of a "blue economy" has arisen as a call to saddle the capability of seaside and marine assets for supportable turn of events. It tries to guarantee that the advantages of seaside trade are fairly dispersed, encouraging comprehensive development that inspires networks along the shores.

The essences of seaside trade are not restricted to the land; they reach out to the profundities of the sea. The oceanic business, with its armada of vessels going from compartment boats to fishing boats, frames the foundation of seaside economies. The angler projecting his net at first light off the shore of Hokkaido is as much a piece of the story as the chief exploring a supertanker through the blocked waters of the Singapore Waterway. The sea labor force, different and interconnected, structures a local area that traverses the globe.

In the unpredictable dance of beach front trade, the job of guideline and administration is crucial. The Worldwide Oceanic Association (IMO), with its order to manage transporting at the worldwide level, assumes a focal part in guaranteeing the wellbeing, security, and natural maintainability of sea exercises. Deals and shows, from the Unified Countries Show on the Law of the Ocean (UNCLOS) to provincial arrangements, give the legitimate system that oversees the perplexing snare of exercises that unfurl along the shorelines of the world.

The meaning of waterfront trade isn't lost on policymakers, who perceive the capability of seaside regions as motors of monetary development. Coordinated waterfront the board tries to orchestrate the contending requests on beach front assets, adjusting the goals of financial improvement with the basic to safeguard the delicate seaside environments. The difficulties are multi-layered, requiring a nuanced approach that considers the intricacies of both human exercises and regular cycles.

In the journey for economical beach front trade, the idea of blue advancement has acquired unmistakable quality. It includes a range of innovative headways and intelligent fixes pointed toward outfitting the capability of the sea while limiting the ecological effect. From seaward wind cultivates that saddle the force of the breeze to desalination advances that address water shortage, blue development addresses a guarantee to a future where success coincides with ecological stewardship.

The stories of beach front business are additionally accounts of flexibility. Beach front networks, enduring the hardships of monetary changes and natural difficulties, exemplify the soul of transformation. Directly following cataclysmic events, for example, tropical storms and tidal waves, these networks ascend from the garbage, modifying their lives and occupations. The flexibility of beach front business is a demonstration of the dauntless human soul, which tracks down strength even with misfortune and draws motivation from the everlasting beat of the tides.

In the multifaceted embroidery of beach front business, social personality is entwined with monetary action. The waterfront urban communities of Morocco, with their energetic business sectors and twisted medinas, mirror the rich embroidered artwork of North African legacy. The fragrance of flavors, the energetic shades of materials, and the cadenced beats of customary music combine to make an air that is both a festival of social character and a demonstration of the persevering through tradition of waterfront exchange.

The specialty of shipbuilding, an old art that has developed over centuries, is a living demonstration of the resourcefulness of beach front networks. From the wooden dhows of the Bedouin Inlet to the smooth compartment boats of East Asia, every vessel bears the engraving of social customs and mechanical advancement. Shipyards, where the hints of mallets on steel resound with the murmurs of the ocean breeze, are the pots where the fantasies of sea investigation and exchange come to fruition.

In the domain of waterfront business, the idea of "blue the travel industry" has arisen as a practical choice to mass the travel industry. It urges explorers to draw in with seaside biological systems in a capable way, encouraging an appreciation for the fragile harmony between human movement and the regular habitat. From coral reef protection tasks to local area based eco-the travel industry drives, blue the travel industry looks to make a cooperative connection among the travel industry and the safeguarding of beach front assets.

The sea space, frequently described by its endlessness and apparently unlimited skylines, isn't safe to the international flows that shape the world. Key chokepoints, for example, the Waterway of Hormuz and the South China Ocean, give testimony regarding the complicated interchange of public interests and worldwide business. The opportunity of route, cherished in worldwide regulation, is a foundation of seaside business, guaranteeing that the corridors of worldwide exchange stay open and unhampered.

The stories of seaside business are accounts of association and union. The old nautical civilizations, from the Phoenicians to the Polynesians, established the groundworks for a world associated by water. The Silk Street, with its sea branches, worked with the trading of products and thoughts across landmasses. Today, the idea of a "blue belt" imagines an organization of marine safeguarded regions that rises above public limits, making a common obligation to the conservation of the sea's biodiversity.

In the contemporary period, the computerized unrest has led to the idea of "brilliant ports" that influence innovation to upgrade productivity and manageability. From robotized holder terminals to blockchain-based store network the executives, these mechanical advancements are reshaping the scene of waterfront business.

The port representing things to come isn't simply a center for the actual trade of merchandise however a powerful biological system where information and network drive the following flood of financial change.

The draw of beach front trade isn't restricted to the sunlight hours; it reaches out to the nighttime domain where the lights of waterfront urban communities sparkle like gems against the scenery of the ocean. The night gatekeeper on a holder transport, exploring through the murkiness with the guide of complex route frameworks, is a cutting edge watchman of the oceanic domain. The waterfront urban communities, with their enlightened horizons, recount an account of human creativity and strength that rises above the limits of existence.

As we explore the rich embroidery of seaside trade, it becomes obvious that the story isn't static; it is a no nonsense element formed by the flows of history, innovation, and the indigenous habitat. From the old ports of times long past to the modern brilliant ports of tomorrow, the development of beach front business is a demonstration of the versatile soul of mankind. The essences of beach front trade, various and interconnected, mirror the bunch manners by which human inventiveness has bridled the capability of the seaside scene.

All in all, the representations of beach front trade illustrate the interconnectedness of human development with the huge region of the sea. From the clamoring ports that stand as passages to the world to the peaceful fishing towns that exemplify an immortal association with the ocean, the beach front scene is a material on which the stories of exchange, industry, and social trade unfurl. As we explore the mind boggling flows of the oceanic space, the essences of seaside business uncover the unique transaction of custom and development, strength and variation. In this steadily developing embroidered artwork, the account of waterfront trade keeps on being composed, formed by the yearnings and attempts of the people who find their livelihoods and dreams along the shores where land meets ocean.

Chapter 1

Setting Sail

In our current reality where the limits among the real world and creative mind are basically as liquid as the tides that oversee an epic immense seas, the excursion starts. A solitary figure remains on the climate beaten moors, looking out at the skyline where the sky meets the ocean in a consistent dance of purplish blue tints. The pungent breeze conveys murmurs of far off lands and untold undertakings, touching off a flash in the spirit of the vagabond.

The harbors, worn by the endless comings and goings of boats, reverberation with the historical backdrop of oceanic endeavors. Wooden boards squeak underneath as the explorer pushes toward the vessel that will act as a conductor to unfamiliar regions. The boat, a magnificent behemoth with surging sails that get the breeze's hug, weaves tenderly in the harbor. Its body, scarred by the fights pursued against whirlwinds and time, demonstrates the veracity of the flexibility of the people who try to challenge the unexplored world.

As the explorer ventures onto the deck, the air murmurs with expectation. Group individuals, a different outfit of people with stories carved on their countenances, rush about like honey bees getting ready for a fantastic undertaking. The chief, an endured veteran of the oceans, stands tall in charge, his eyes holding onto the insight of innumerable nautical miles. His voice, a profound tone that deserves both admiration and brotherhood, rings out as he gives orders that slice through the encompassing orchestra of nautical life.

The boat's sails spread out with a musical effortlessness, slowing down to rest and pushing the vessel forward into the extraordinary unexplored world. The explorer, presently a piece of this marine society, feels the beat of the boat underneath their feet. The consistent beat of the waves lapping against the frame turns into a heartbeat, synchronizing with the aggregate heartbeat of the group. A bond is produced in the cauldron of common perspective, an implicit consent to confront anything that difficulties lie ahead as one.

Days transform into evenings, and evenings into days, as the boat outlines its course across the vast spread of the untamed ocean. Every dawn carries with it the commitment of new revelations, while every nightfall paints the sky in tints of red hot orange and violet, a demonstration of the persevering through magnificence that graces even the most barren corners of the world. The group, when outsiders, presently shares chuckling and stories around the gleaming sparkle of the boat's lamps.

The journey isn't without its preliminaries. Storms, wild and unwavering, test the grit of both the boat and its group. Waves, huge in their level, run into the vessel, taking steps to overwhelm it in the pit. However, similar to a phoenix coming to life, the boat rises out of the whirlwind battered yet whole. The team, endured by the tempest's wrath, wears their strength like a respectable symbol.

In the midst of the difficulties, the ocean uncovers its mysteries. Bioluminescent animals enlighten the evening, projecting an ethereal sparkle that changes the sea into a divine material. Whales break the surface, their great structures an indication of the sensational power that lives underneath the waves. Islands, covered in fog and secret, coax from the skyline, promising neglected scenes and secret fortunes.

The excursion isn't exclusively an actual one; it is a journey of self-disclosure. The explorer, when restricted by the recognizable shores of schedule, presently remains on the slope of change. The untamed ocean reflects the endlessness of the spirit, welcoming thoughtfulness and disclosure. Dreams and goals, similar to stars in the night sky, guide the way forward, filling in as signals in obscurity.

As the boat sails on, it experiences different vessels — some agreeable, trading stories and supplies, while others bear the markings of robbery, requesting tolls for safe section. Each experience, whether kindhearted or ill-disposed, adds one more layer to the woven artwork of the excursion.

The ocean, fair in its endlessness, turns into a phase where the human show unfurls, where partnerships are manufactured, and where the unstoppable soul of mankind conflicts with the erratic powers of nature.

Amidst the journey, an unconventional island arises not too far off. Its shores are enhanced with lavish vegetation, and the air conveys the sweet scent of outlandish blossoms. The group, drawn by the appeal of the obscure, chooses to make landfall. As they set foot on the island, they find a development dissimilar to any they have experienced previously. The islanders, with skin tanned by the sun and eyes that mirror the insight of ages, greet the explorers wholeheartedly.

The island uncovers itself as a shelter of old information and failed to remember shrewdness. The occupants, capable in the otherworldly expressions, share their bits of knowledge with the team, unwinding the secrets of the universe and the interconnectedness, everything being equal. The voyager, lowered by the significance of these lessons, tracks down a more profound comprehension of their spot in the great embroidery of presence.

In the core of the island, a consecrated forest calls, its trees standing tall as sentinels of time. The air gleams with an extraordinary energy, and murmurs of the past and future entwine. The group, directed by the islanders, participates in a function that rises above the limits of the actual domain. In this ethereal dance of spirits, the limits between individual spirits obscure, and a shared mindset arises.

The island, however an impermanent rest, turns into a urgent section in the continuous adventure of the journey. The information acquired, similar to a valuable freight, is conveyed on board the boat as it heads out again. The explorer, presently improved by the island's insight, turns into an overseer of the esoteric insider facts that will shape the course of the excursion.

As the boat proceeds with its odyssey, the team experiences a peculiarity that challenges the laws of nature. A giant whirlpool, a vortex of basic energy, beats in the core of the ocean. The commander, his eyes mirroring a blend of fear and assurance, chooses to explore through this bedlam, accepting that it holds the way in to a domain past the known.

The boat is brought into the twirling chasm, and reality twists around it. The team, suspended between universes, witnesses dreamlike scenes and strange creatures that oppose depiction. Time itself turns into a slippery idea as the boat navigates aspects, directed by a concealed power. It is an excursion into the magical, a dive into the grandiose flows that weave the texture of the real world.

Arising on the opposite side, the boat winds up in a domain immaculate by the progression of time. Divine bodies, suspended in a dance of unending movement, enlighten a scene that rises above the constraints of mortal discernment.

The team, presently taking the stand concerning the grand, understands that they have passed a boundary into a domain where the limits between the material and the irrelevant are obscured.

In this ethereal domain, the boat experiences creatures of unadulterated energy, elements that exist past the bounds of actual structure. These vast gatekeepers, old and astute, uncover the motivation behind the journey — an odyssey across the expanses of the world as well as through the grandiose flows that tight spot the universe together. The boat, they make sense of, is a vessel of greatness, a course for the investigation of domains outside the ability to grasp of standard humans.

Directed by the inestimable watchmen, the boat sets out on a heavenly journey. It crosses undefined mists that shine with the shades of 1,000 systems, sails through the enormous breezes that convey the murmurs of far off stars, and explores through heavenly flows that interface the embroidery of the universe. The group, presently receptive to the infinite frequencies, encounters a significant solidarity with the universe.

As the boat sails through the infinite immeasurability, it experiences divine peculiarities that challenge natural creative mind. Dark openings, as vast doors, entice with the charm of the unexplored world. Clouds, huge and ethereal, paint the enormous material with dynamic tones. The team, lowered by the grandness of the universe, comprehends that their process rises above the limits of a solitary lifetime.

Amidst the grandiose odyssey, the boat experiences a divine city suspended in the void. Its towers reach toward the sky, and its roads are cleared with stardust. The occupants of this ethereal city, creatures of unadulterated light and energy, welcome the group as close companions. The city, they make sense of, is a nexus of inestimable energies, a combination point for creatures from all edges of the universe.

In the core of the heavenly city, the team finds a vault of general information — a document that narratives the chronicles of civic establishments that have risen and fallen, the insight of enormous sages, and the secrets of the universe. The voyager, presently a searcher of grandiose bits of insight, dives into the vast library of the universe, unwinding the insider facts of presence.

The enormous visit, however ageless in its substance, in the end drives the boat back to the natural waters of the natural domain. The team, presently illuminated by the vast disclosures, gets back to the human plane with a significant comprehension of their spot in the excellent embroidery of creation. The boat, loaded down with the fortunes of grandiose insight, sails toward the skyline where the sky meets the ocean.

The excursion, however set apart by hardships, turns into a demonstration of the unstoppable soul of investigation. The explorer, when a lone figure on the harbors, presently remains as a harbinger of grandiose bits of knowledge, a signal for the individuals who set out to head out into the unfamiliar waters of the unexplored world. The boat, endured by the progression of time and imbued with the energies of far off domains, turns into a vessel of both natural and enormous importance.

Yet again as the boat moors, the group lands, their appearances carved with the insight of the inestimable journey. The skipper, with a look that mirrors the profundities of the universe, gestures in quiet affirmation of the extraordinary excursion.

1.1 Introduction to coastal commerce and its historical significance

Waterfront business, an embroidery woven through the chronicles of mankind's set of experiences, arises as a demonstration of the inventiveness and undertaking of oceanic civilizations. The shores, where the land meets the ocean, have filled in as normal courses for exchange, encouraging monetary thriving, social trade, and the development of social orders. This acquaintance looks for with unwind the rich authentic meaning of beach front business, following its beginnings, advancement, and getting through influence on the course of human progress.

From days of yore, seaside districts have been center points of human movement. The closeness to the ocean blessed these regions with an abundance of assets, from plentiful fisheries to fruitful seaside fields, establishing the groundwork for early settlements. As people group thrived along the coastlines, a cooperative relationship with the ocean started to shape the fate of these seaside occupants. The back and forth movement of the tides reflected the recurrent rhythms of life, impacting food as well as the rise of simple exchange organizations.

The approach of marine vessels denoted a significant crossroads throughout the entire existence of beach front trade. Early mariners, pushed by the breezes and directed by the stars, wandered past the natural sight of the shoreline, growing the skylines of exchange. The Mediterranean, with its interconnected organization of old civic establishments, saw the ascent of sea shipping lanes that associated the Phoenicians, Greeks, Egyptians, and other nautical societies. The trading of products, thoughts, and advancements along these oceanic interstates laid the foundation for the thriving city-expresses that dabbed the Mediterranean scene.

In the Far East, the oceanic Silk Street arose as a course for exchange between the East and the West. Chinese trashes explored the immense field of the South China Ocean, associating with nautical countries in Southeast Asia, the Indian subcontinent, and the Bedouin Landmass. Flavors, silks, valuable metals, and different products navigated the oceanic Silk Street, connecting assorted societies and encouraging the cross-fertilization of thoughts and customs.

As middle age Europe introduced the period of investigation, waterfront business took on new aspects. The Period of Disclosure saw European powers competing for control of worthwhile shipping lanes, prompting the circumnavigation of the globe by fearless adventurers like Ferdinand Magellan. The mission for direct ocean courses to the flavor rich Indies and the legendary terrains of riches and opportunity prodded a sea race that reshaped the international scene.

Beach front urban areas like Venice, Genoa, and Amsterdam became focal points of exchange, collecting abundance and impacting the course of world occasions. The ascent of oceanic domains, including the Portuguese, Spanish, Dutch, and English, was inseparably connected to their command over waterfront shipping lanes. The foundation of provinces and general stores along far off shores energized the commercial aspirations of these nautical countries.

The Time of Sail, described by superb tall boats with surging sails, embodied the peak of seaside business. The Atlantic slave exchange, a dim section in mankind's set of experiences, took the stand concerning the transportation of millions of oppressed people across the misleading waters, connecting the landmasses in a grievous trap of double-dealing. Sugar, tobacco, cotton, and different items streamed across the Atlantic, changing waterfront locales into financial forces to be reckoned with.

The Modern Upset, a seismic change in financial and mechanical ideal models, further catalyzed the development of beach front business. Steamships, moved by the force of steam motors, supplanted conventional cruising vessels, reforming transportation and exchange. Seaside urban areas with admittance to safe streams and profound harbors expanded into modern focuses, working with the development of unrefined substances and completed merchandise.

The development of railroads and interconnected transportation networks additionally supplemented waterfront business. Seaside urban communities, presently associated with hinterlands through a snare of railways and waterways, became significant hubs in the worldwide store network. Ports, when passages to sea exchange, advanced into dynamic centers of parcel, working with the consistent exchange of merchandise among land and ocean.

The twentieth century saw the ascent of containerization, a change in perspective that reformed waterfront business. Normalized holders, effectively adaptable between boats, trucks, and trains, smoothed out planned operations and diminished the time and cost of moving merchandise. Waterfront ports, furnished with present day compartment terminals, became imperative gear-teeth in the worldwide exchange hardware, dealing with monstrous volumes of freight with exceptional productivity.

The beach front trade of the cutting edge time is described by a perplexing interaction of monetary, international, and ecological elements. Globalization has interconnected economies, making seaside locales urgent players in the elements of worldwide exchange. Seaside urban areas, with their deepwater ports and vital areas, have become passages to territorial and worldwide business sectors.

The natural effect of waterfront trade has gone under investigation as worries about contamination, territory obliteration, and environmental change have acquired unmistakable quality. The transportation of merchandise via ocean, while proficient, has added to marine contamination through oil slicks, balance water release, and the arrival of poisons. Seaside biological systems, fragile and different, endure the worst part of these natural difficulties, requiring feasible practices in oceanic exchange.

The verifiable meaning of seaside business stretches out past financial aspects and exchange. It has formed the social embroidery of seaside networks, impacting workmanship, cooking, language, and social traditions. Seaside urban communities, with their mixed mix of impacts from far off shores, stand as living demonstrations of the persevering through tradition of sea exchange. The trading of thoughts and social practices along beach front courses has improved the human experience, encouraging an embroidery of variety that rises above geological limits.

In the contemporary setting, waterfront business keeps on assuming a crucial part in the worldwide economy. Megacities arranged along shorelines, like New York, Tokyo, and Shanghai, are monetary forces to be reckoned with that drive advancement, money, and innovation. Waterfront areas act as unique centers for ventures going from transportation and operations to the travel industry and sustainable power.

Innovative progressions, including robotization, man-made consciousness, and digitalization, are reshaping the scene of waterfront trade. Savvy ports furnished with state of the art advancements enhance freight taking care of, route, and security. Automated flying vehicles (UAVs) and independent vessels are ready to change

Portraits Of Coastal Commerce

the effectiveness and security of oceanic transportation, proclaiming another period in beach front business.

The difficulties confronting waterfront trade in the 21st century are diverse. Environmental change represents a danger to beach front framework, with rising ocean levels and outrageous climate occasions endangering the security of ports and transportation courses. International strains and sea debates can possibly upset worldwide exchange, influencing beach front locales that depend on the free progression of products.

Ecological supportability is arising as a point of convergence for the fate of seaside trade. The oceanic business is investigating cleaner and more economical drive advancements, including electric and half breed vessels.

Developments in transport plan and eco-friendliness expect to moderate the natural effect of sea transportation, lining up with worldwide endeavors to progress toward an additional practical and versatile future.

All in all, the set of experiences and meaning of seaside business are entwined with the actual texture of human civilization. From the earliest seaside settlements to the complex sea organizations of the cutting edge period, the shores have been the two observers and modelers of financial, social, and innovative advancement. Waterfront business, with its bunch features, stays a powerful power that shapes the fate of countries, impacts social trade, and pushes mankind toward new skylines. As we explore the flows of the 21st 100 years, the tale of beach front trade keeps on unfurling, repeating the immortal cadence of the tides that have directed human undertakings for centuries.

1.2 Overview of key coastal trading routes and their impact on global economies

The world's waterfront exchanging courses structure a huge and complex organization, interfacing landmasses and working with the trading of merchandise, thoughts, and societies. These sea conduits play had an essential impact in forming the course of worldwide economies since forever ago. This outline dives into some key seaside exchanging courses, investigating their beginnings, importance, and getting through influence on the interconnected snare of global exchange.

One of the most established and most generally critical beach front exchanging courses is the Oceanic Silk Street. Beginning in old China, this oceanic course worked with exchange between the East and the West, connecting the prosperous Chinese lines with the way of life of Southeast Asia, South Asia, the Center East, and ultimately Europe. The Sea Silk Street, interlaced with its overland partner, worked with the trading of silk, flavors, valuable metals, and social impacts along its broad organization of ports and exchanging centers.

The Mediterranean Ocean, encompassed by three mainlands — Europe, Asia, and Africa — has been a support of civilization and a nexus of seaside exchange for centuries. The Phoenicians, famous sailors and brokers, laid out an organization of oceanic courses interfacing the Mediterranean's different societies. The city-territories of Athens, Rome, and later Venice and Genoa, flourished as oceanic powers, affecting exchange, governmental issues, and culture across the Mediterranean bowl.

The Indian Sea, frequently alluded to as the "zest course," was another basic waterfront exchanging network that associated the East with the West. Middle Easterner brokers explored the Indian Sea, connecting the Bedouin Promontory with the Indian subcontinent, East Africa, and Southeast Asia. The trading of flavors, materials, and valuable stones along the Indian Sea shipping lanes assumed a vital part in molding the economies of civilizations like the Bedouin Caliphates and the sea domains of Southeast Asia.

The Atlantic Slave Exchange, while a dull section ever, was a huge waterfront exchanging course that significantly influenced the economies of Africa, Europe, and the Americas. Ships loaded down with subjugated people cruised from the West African coast to the Americas, where they were constrained in the process of childbirth on estates. The three-sided shipping lanes connected Europe, Africa, and the Americas, with merchandise like materials, guns, and rum traded for subjugated people in Africa, who were then moved to the Americas, where the cycle proceeded.

The Time of Investigation in the fifteenth and sixteenth hundreds of years achieved the foundation of new seaside exchanging courses. European powers looked for direct ocean courses to the wealth of Asia, prompting the revelation of new grounds and the circumnavigation of the globe. Christopher Columbus' journeys across the Atlantic, Vasco da Gama's excursion around the Cape of Good Expectation, and Ferdinand Magellan's circumnavigation of the Earth opened up new sea courses, reshaping the elements of worldwide exchange.

The Pacific Sea, the world's biggest and most profound sea, turned into a point of convergence for investigation and beach front exchange. Spanish ships, part of the Manila-Acapulco ship exchange, crossed the huge breadth of the Pacific, interfacing the Philippines with Mexico. This transoceanic shipping lane worked with the trading of merchandise like silk, flavors, and valuable metals, impacting the economies of both the Spanish Domain and East Asia.

In the nineteenth hundred years, the launch of the Suez Waterway in 1869 changed oceanic exchange by giving an immediate course between the Mediterranean and Red Oceans. This fake stream, slicing through the Isthmus of Suez, fundamentally abbreviated the journey from Europe to Asia. Beach front shipping lanes through the Suez Trench became basic for European powers, especially those with provinces in Asia, as they looked for quicker and more productive admittance to the assets of the East.

The Panama Waterway, initiated in 1914, likewise changed worldwide exchange by associating the Atlantic and Pacific Seas. Ships cruising from the East Bank of the Americas toward the West Coast — as well as the other way around — at this point not expected to embrace the extensive and risky excursion around the southern tip of South America. The Panama Trench turned into a crucial easy route for oceanic exchange, decreasing travel times and fuel utilization.

The rise of containerization during the twentieth century further altered waterfront exchanging courses. Normalized holders, effectively adaptable between boats, trucks, and trains, smoothed out strategies and empowered the proficient development of merchandise. Waterfront ports outfitted with compartment terminals became vital hubs in the worldwide store network, working with the fast and savvy move of freight.

One of the most basic contemporary seaside exchanging courses is the East Asian sea passage, connecting the assembling forces to be reckoned with of East Asia with business sectors all over the planet. China, specifically, has turned into a worldwide monetary force to be reckoned with, and its seaside exchanging courses are instrumental in the development of products to and from significant ports like Shanghai, Shenzhen, and Hong Kong. These courses interface East Asia with Europe, Africa, and the Americas, contributing fundamentally to the worldwide economy.

The Cold Sea, once blocked because of ice, is acquiring consideration as a potential new waterfront exchanging course. The liquefying of Icy ice because of environmental change has opened up the chance of more limited ocean courses interfacing Europe and Asia. The Northern Ocean Course, along the Russian Icy coast, has seen expanded sea action, in spite of the fact that difficulties, for example, ice conditions, framework, and ecological worries should be addressed for its maximum capacity to be understood.

The effect of beach front exchanging courses on worldwide economies is diverse and significant. These courses work with the development of merchandise, unrefined components, and fabricated items, interfacing makers with shoppers on a worldwide scale. The effectiveness of waterfront shipping lanes straightforwardly impacts the expense of products, influencing evaluating elements in business sectors around the world. The openness and traversability of these courses likewise assume an essential part in deciding the seriousness of seaside urban communities and locales in the worldwide economy.

Seaside exchanging courses contribute essentially to the financial improvement of beach front urban areas and locales. Ports, filling in as doors to oceanic exchange, become central focuses for monetary movement, producing work, income, and foundation advancement. Urban communities decisively situated along major seaside shipping lanes, like Singapore, Rotterdam, and Los Angeles, arise as vital participants in the worldwide economy, with flourishing coordinated operations, delivery, and exchange related ventures.

The interconnectedness of waterfront exchanging courses encourages financial association among countries. Countries with broad shorelines and advanced sea framework influence their geographic benefits to become fundamental players in provincial and worldwide exchange. This relationship, while encouraging participation, can likewise prompt international strains as countries compete for command over vital oceanic chokepoints and shipping lanes.

The social effect of seaside exchanging courses is significant, as these pathways of business work with the trading of thoughts, dialects, and customs. Seaside urban areas, generally blends of social variety, become pots where various societies meet and combine. The cosmopolitan idea of seaside networks is much of the time an impression of the different impacts achieved by hundreds of years of oceanic exchange.

While beach front exchanging courses have been instrumental in driving monetary development and social trade, they are not without challenges. Robbery, especially in districts like the Bay of Aden and the Waterway of Malacca, represents a danger to sea security and disturbs exchange streams. International pressures, regional debates, and the potential for struggle along essential sea courses can have sweeping ramifications for worldwide exchange.

Natural supportability is a developing worry with regards to seaside exchanging courses. The transportation business, a spine of sea exchange, is a huge supporter of air and water contamination. The counterbalance water release from ships, oil slicks, and emanations from sea transport unfavorably affect beach front environments. Endeavors to moderate the natural effect of waterfront exchange incorporate the improvement of cleaner impetus advancements, stricter ecological guidelines, and drives to advance feasible delivery rehearses.

1.3 The role of ports and coastal cities in facilitating trade and commerce

The job of ports and beach front urban communities in working with exchange and business is major to the elements of the worldwide economy. These sea entryways act as fundamental hubs in the many-sided organization of global exchange, interfacing makers and purchasers across mainlands. This investigation dives into the complex elements of ports and seaside urban communities, looking at their verifiable advancement, financial importance, and the difficulties and open doors they face in a consistently developing universe of exchange.

By and large, ports have been fundamental to the advancement of waterfront urban communities, going about as points of interaction among land and ocean. The earliest settlements arose along riverbanks and shorelines, where the accessibility of water worked with transportation and exchange. As human social orders developed, so did the significance of ports, which became center points for sea trade, social trade, and monetary development.

Waterfront urban areas, invested with normal harbors or decisively created ports, arose as flourishing focuses of exchange and financial movement. The old city of Tire, situated on the Mediterranean coast, was famous for its sea ability and filled in as a key port in the Phoenician exchanging realm. Essentially, Venice, arranged on an organization of islands in the Adriatic Ocean, turned into a sea force to be reckoned with during the Medieval times, interfacing East and West through its clamoring port.

Portraits Of Coastal Commerce

The financial meaning of ports and beach front urban areas is attached in their ability to work with the development of merchandise. Ports act as parcel focuses, where freight is moved between various methods of transportation — ships, trucks, trains — empowering the consistent progression of merchandise along the production network. The productivity of port tasks straightforwardly impacts the expense and speed of shipping merchandise, affecting the seriousness of beach front urban areas in the worldwide commercial center.

Seaside urban areas, with their closeness to ports, become key areas for ventures and organizations engaged with worldwide exchange. The grouping of delivery organizations, strategies suppliers, customs organizations, and other exchange related ventures around ports makes sea bunches, encouraging cooperation and proficiency. These groups, frequently alluded to as sea modern buildings, add to the monetary energy of waterfront urban communities and improve their part in the worldwide exchange organization.

The development of ports from straightforward harbor offices to modern multimodal centers has been a characterizing part of their job in exchange and trade. Current ports are furnished with cutting edge foundation, including holder terminals, robotized freight taking care of frameworks, and multi-purpose associations. Containerization, a progressive improvement in sea transport, normalized freight taking care of and changed ports into high-limit offices equipped for dealing with enormous volumes of products.

Compartment terminals, highlighting transcending cranes and heaps of normalized holders, are at the very front of present day port activities. These terminals empower the quick stacking and dumping of containerized freight from ships, giving a smoothed out process that limits completion times. The presentation of advancements like computerized directed vehicles (AGVs) and radio-recurrence distinguishing proof (RFID) further improves the proficiency of compartment taking care of in ports.

The availability of ports to hinterlands through street, rail, and inland stream networks is a vital calculate their viability as exchange facilitators. Ports that are all around coordinated into multimodal transportation frameworks become passages to broad hinterlands, giving productive admittance to business sectors and conveyance focuses. Waterfront urban areas with advanced transportation foundation, including vicinity to significant roadways and rail organizations, upgrade the allure of their ports for exchange and strategies exercises.

The essential situating of ports along significant delivery courses assumes a vital part in their effect on worldwide business. Ports arranged at key sea junction, for example, the Singapore Waterway, the Panama Channel, or the Suez Trench, become basic hubs in worldwide transportation organizations. These chokepoints, where significant delivery paths meet, impact the productivity and cost-adequacy of oceanic exchange, making the related ports central members in forming worldwide exchange designs.

The financial effect of ports on beach front urban areas reaches out past the immediate income created by port tasks. Ports invigorate neighborhood economies by setting out work open doors, supporting subordinate ventures, and drawing in speculation. The multiplier impact of port-related exercises can prompt the advancement of port urban communities into flourishing metropolitan habitats with assorted economies. Urban areas like Singapore, Rotterdam, and Shanghai owe quite a bit of their monetary conspicuousness to the essential situating and proficiency of their ports.

The job of ports as impetuses for local improvement is exemplified by the idea of deregulation zones and exceptional monetary zones (SEZs). These zones, frequently situated inside or in nearness to ports, offer good circumstances for organizations, like duty motivators, smoothed out guidelines, and upgraded framework. Waterfront urban areas influence the presence of these zones to draw in unfamiliar direct venture (FDI) and advance product situated businesses, encouraging monetary development and occupation creation.

The voyage business addresses one more aspect of the connection among ports and seaside urban areas. Ports with traveler terminals take special care of the flourishing journey the travel industry area, inviting huge number of travelers every year. Beach front urban communities decisively situated along famous voyage courses benefit from the monetary convergence created by journey transport visits. The travel industry, containing lodgings, cafés, and amusement administrations, flourishes couple with the voyage area, adding to the financial variety of waterfront urban communities.

Ecological manageability has arisen as a basic thought in the turn of events and activity of ports. As key hubs in worldwide exchange, ports add to ecological difficulties like air and water contamination, natural surroundings debasement, and ozone harming substance emanations. Endeavors to moderate the natural effect of ports incorporate the reception of cleaner advances, the utilization of shore power for docked vessels, and the execution of eco-accommodating port framework.

The idea of green ports underscores naturally cognizant practices in port activities. Green ports focus on energy proficiency, discharge decrease, and the utilization of sustainable power sources. Drives like jolt of port gear, execution of energy-effective lighting, and the reception of supportable development materials add to the advancement of harmless to the ecosystem port offices.

The difficulties looked by ports and beach front urban communities are assorted and dynamic. Foundation blockage, brought about by the rising volume of worldwide exchange, can strain the limit of ports and obstruct productive freight development. The extension and updating of port foundation, including holder terminals, compartments, and street and rail associations, become basic to satisfy the developing needs of worldwide exchange.

Port security is a foremost worry with regards to worldwide exchange. Ports are helpless against security dangers, including psychological warfare, robbery, and the carrying of illegal products. Carrying out powerful safety efforts, for example, the utilization of cutting edge reconnaissance advances, access control frameworks, and cooperation with policing, is essential to protecting port activities and keeping up with the honesty of supply chains.

The digitization of oceanic exchange, frequently alluded to as Sea 4.0, presents the two open doors and difficulties for ports and waterfront urban communities. Advanced innovations, including blockchain, the Web of Things (IoT), and man-made brainpower (artificial intelligence), offer the possibility to upgrade the effectiveness and straightforwardness of port activities. Nonetheless, the reception of these advancements requires huge interests in computerized foundation and online protection to moderate possible dangers.

Worldwide international elements likewise influence the job of ports and beach front urban communities in exchange and trade. Oceanic debates, regional cases, and political strains can disturb the smooth progression of merchandise through key transportation courses. Ports situated in politically delicate areas might confront vulnerabilities that influence their engaging quality as exchange entryways. Exploring international difficulties requires a nuanced comprehension of worldwide relations and vital preparation by port specialists and beach front city pioneers.

The eventual fate of ports and seaside urban communities in working with exchange and business lies their capacity to adjust to advancing patterns and difficulties. The ascent of online business, changes in shopper conduct, and changes in worldwide store network elements are reshaping the scene of global exchange. Ports that embrace mechanical developments, put resources into reasonable practices, and cultivate coordinated effort with partners are better situated to flourish in this powerful climate.

Mechanization and digitalization are ready to change port tasks before very long. Independent vessels, shrewd holder terminals, and information driven dynamic cycles are supposed to upgrade the productivity and unwavering quality of port exercises. The idea of brilliant ports, where interconnected innovations upgrade each part of port tasks, addresses the fate of exchange help.

The development of the Cold delivery courses because of environmental change opens up additional opportunities for ports in northern districts. The Northern Ocean Course, along the Russian Cold coast, and the Northwest Entry, through the Canadian Icy Archipelago, present more limited courses among Europe and Asia. In any case, the difficulties of exploring frosty waters, absence of foundation, and natural worries should be tended.

Working with exchange and trade is an intricate and dynamic interaction that includes a horde of interconnected components, from effective transportation organizations and operations to the essential situating of ports, the development of computerized innovations, and the job of government strategies. This complex framework is the foundation of the worldwide economy, affecting the development of products, encouraging monetary development, and molding the interconnectedness of countries. This investigation dives into the critical parts and difficulties of working with exchange and business, disentangling the perplexing embroidered artwork that supports the progression of merchandise across borders.

At the core of exchange assistance lies the framework that empowers the smooth development of merchandise. Transportation organizations, incorporating streets, rail routes, aviation routes, and streams, structure the actual conductors for the trading of items among makers and purchasers. Advanced framework decreases transportation costs, limits travel times, and improves the general effectiveness of supply chains.

Ports, filling in as connection points among land and ocean, assume an essential part in exchange help. These sea passages are basic hubs in the worldwide production network, associating transporting courses and working with the parcel of merchandise. The essential situating of ports impacts exchange designs, and the development of these offices from conventional harbors to current, mechanically progressed center points mirrors the continuous change of exchange and trade.

Productive port tasks are critical for exchange help, and containerization has been a progressive improvement in such manner. Normalized holders, effectively adaptable between various methods of transportation, have smoothed out freight dealing with processes. Compartment terminals outfitted with trend setting innovations, like mechanized cranes and global positioning frameworks, improve the stacking and dumping of vessels, decreasing times required to circle back and upgrading by and large port proficiency.

Besides, the combination of computerized innovations has introduced another period of exchange assistance. The idea of Exchange Help 4.0, described by the digitization of cycles and the utilization of advancements, for example, blockchain, man-made reasoning (artificial intelligence), and the Web of Things (IoT), is reshaping the way in which exchange is led. These innovations upgrade straightforwardness, decrease desk work, and give ongoing perceivability into the development of products, accordingly limiting deferrals and working on the dependability of supply chains.

Customs strategies and documentation assume a urgent part in exchange help. Disentangling and smoothing out these cycles using computerized stages and orchestrated norms add to the proficiency of cross-line exchange. Single-window frameworks, where dealers can present all necessary documentation through a bound together point of interaction, diminish regulatory obstacles and work with quicker leeway of merchandise at borders.

Government arrangements and guidelines altogether influence exchange help. Customs obligations, levies, and non-tax hindrances impact the expense and simplicity of carrying on with work across borders. Economic alliance, like international alliances (FTAs) and provincial exchange coalitions, mean to diminish obstructions and advance the free progression of products between partaking countries. Notwithstanding, exploring the perplexing snare of global exchange guidelines stays a test for organizations took part in cross-line trade.

Framework improvement is a critical driver of exchange help. Interest in current transportation organizations, including roadways, railroads, and air terminals, upgrades availability and diminishes the expenses related with the development of merchandise. In the sea space, the extension and overhauling of ports, as well as the advancement of proficient inland stream frameworks, add to the general viability of exchange help.

Key topographical situating is one more basic component in the assistance of exchange and business. Nations and urban areas situated at key intersection of worldwide shipping lanes, like Singapore, Dubai, and Rotterdam, become normal centers for global trade. The effective parcel of merchandise at these essential areas streamlines the worldwide store network and adds to the monetary advancement of these exchange driven districts.

Coordinated operations and store network the board are essential parts of exchange assistance. Proficient coordinated factors guarantee that products arrive at their objective in an ideal and financially savvy way. The advancement of stock administration, dispersion organizations, and transportation courses improves the general adequacy of supply chains. Progresses in innovation, like ongoing following and examination, add to the perceivability and versatility of store network tasks.

Exchange finance assumes a urgent part in working with worldwide exchange, especially for little and medium-sized endeavors (SMEs). Admittance to credit, exchange funding systems, and chance relief apparatuses empower organizations to participate in cross-line exchanges with certainty. Worldwide monetary organizations and exchange finance suppliers assume a fundamental part in supporting organizations by giving the essential monetary instruments to work with exchange.

While exchange assistance brings various advantages, it likewise presents moves that should be tended to. Customs shortcomings, administrative formality, and conflicting administrative practices across lines can block the smooth progression of merchandise. Conflicting or obsolete foundation, both physical and advanced, presents difficulties to the proficiency of exchange assistance processes. Tending to these difficulties requires cooperation among states, confidential area partners, and worldwide associations.

International pressures and exchange debates can likewise upset the assistance of exchange. Duties, assents, and protectionist measures make vulnerabilities for organizations participated in cross-line trade. The goal of such questions and the advancement of a guidelines based worldwide exchanging framework are fundamental for encouraging a climate helpful for exchange assistance.

Ecological supportability is arising as a basic thought in exchange help. The transportation of products, especially via ocean and air, adds to fossil fuel byproducts and ecological debasement.

Drives to advance green coordinated operations, lessen the carbon impression of transportation, and embrace manageable practices in exchange related exercises are building up some forward momentum as a feature of the worldwide work to address environmental change.

The inclusivity of exchange help is likewise a critical thought. Guaranteeing that the advantages of worldwide exchange are shared impartially requires strategies that help the support of SMEs, decrease boundaries for emerging nations, and advance social and natural obligation in worldwide stock chains. Comprehensive exchange help adds to neediness decrease, financial turn of events, and social prosperity.

The job of innovation in exchange assistance keeps on advancing. Blockchain, with its decentralized and secure record framework, holds the possibility to upgrade the straightforwardness and detectability of supply chains. Man-made intelligence applications, including prescient investigation and robotization, add to the streamlining of coordinated operations and customs processes. Proceeded with interest in innovative work is vital for tackle the maximum capacity of these advances for exchange assistance.

The effect of worldwide occasions, like the Coronavirus pandemic, highlights the significance of strength in exchange help. Disturbances to supply chains, travel limitations, and changes in purchaser conduct have featured the requirement for adaptability and versatility in worldwide exchange frameworks. Computerized advancements and possibility arranging assume a pivotal part in building versatility and relieving the effect of unanticipated occasions on global exchange.

All in all, working with exchange and trade is a dynamic and diverse undertaking that requires the coordinated endeavors of states, organizations, and global associations. From the advancement of effective foundation to the reception of computerized innovations and the quest for comprehensive and feasible exchange rehearses, the components of exchange assistance are interconnected and commonly building up. As the world keeps on developing, the continuous change of exchange and trade will depend on development, joint effort, and a guarantee to making a more interconnected and strong worldwide economy.

Chapter 2

The Maritime Marketplace

The oceanic commercial center stands as a powerful crossing point of trade, innovation, and worldwide network. Extending across immense spreads of the World's waters, it winds around an embroidery of exchange that has been essential to the improvement of developments since the beginning of time. As the world has advanced, so too has the oceanic commercial center, adjusting to the moving tides of financial, political, and mechanical change.

At its center, the sea commercial center is a mind boggling organization of businesses and exercises that work with the development of products, individuals, and thoughts across seas and oceans. Boats of different sizes and types, from epic holder vessels to deft fishing boats, explore the waters, framing the foundation of this far reaching worldwide framework. Ports and harbors, going about as clamoring doors, act as basic hubs in the organization, working with the stacking and dumping of freight and offering fundamental types of assistance to the vessels that pass through.

Exchange, a foundation of human development, has been complicatedly connected to oceanic exercises for quite a long time. The oceanic commercial center, with its immense delivery paths and mind boggling supply chains, empowers the trading of merchandise on a scale that rises above lines and landmasses. From the old Silk Street to the advanced delivery paths of the Pacific and Atlantic, oceanic exchange has molded the course of history, encouraging social trade, financial turn of events, and international connections.

In the contemporary period, the oceanic commercial center has arrived at extraordinary degrees of intricacy and refinement. Globalization has enhanced the interconnectivity of economies, making the sea area an essential supply route of worldwide exchange. Huge holder ships, equipped for conveying great many standard-sized compartments, cross the oceans, framing a sea interstate that joins creation focuses with purchaser markets. These vessels, worked by a different exhibit of transportation organizations, exemplify the scale and effectiveness that characterize the cutting edge oceanic commercial center.

The oceanic commercial center, in any case, isn't without its difficulties. Ecological worries, robbery, international strains, and administrative intricacies present impressive hindrances that require imaginative arrangements. The push for manageability has incited the business to investigate elective powers, take on cleaner advancements, and execute rigid natural guidelines. As environmental change strengthens, the oceanic area faces expanding strain to decrease its carbon impression and relieve the ecological effect of its tasks.

Mechanical headways assume a critical part in molding the eventual fate of the sea commercial center. Computerization, man-made reasoning, and digitalization are changing conventional sea works on, offering new efficiencies and capacities. Independent vessels, directed by state of the art route frameworks, address an outskirts that holds the commitment of more secure and more proficient sea transportation. Advanced stages and brilliant innovations work with constant checking of vessels, upgrade course arranging, and improve generally functional proficiency.

The oceanic commercial center isn't exclusively about the development of products; it additionally envelops the vehicle of individuals. Journey ships, ship administrations, and other traveler vessels add to the lively embroidered artwork of oceanic exercises. These vessels give fundamental transportation as well as deal special travel encounters, interfacing individuals and societies across the oceans. The journey business, specifically, has seen critical development, with rich boats becoming drifting retreats that cross the world's seas.

Notwithstanding traveler transport, the sea commercial center assumes a urgent part in supporting seaward exercises. Seaward oil and gas investigation and extraction, sustainable power projects, and submerged link establishments are among the different exercises that depend on oceanic framework. Specific vessels, outfitted with cutting edge innovation, support these tasks, adding to the energy scene and the worldwide network of data.

The sea commercial center is innately worldwide, with delivery courses associating major monetary centers and working with the progression of products on a phenomenal scale. The essential significance of specific oceanic chokepoints, for example, the Suez Trench, the Panama Channel, and the Waterway of Malacca, highlights the international elements of sea exchange. Command over these key entries has been a wellspring of international moving since the beginning of time, featuring the complicated connection between oceanic trade and worldwide power elements.

International contemplations additionally become possibly the most important factor in the turn of events and support of maritime powers. Naval forces all over the planet assume a double part in shielding oceanic shipping lanes and stating public interests. The capacity to extend power across the oceans has for quite some time been a proportion of a country's international impact. Maritime presence stops likely dangers as well as guarantees the security of indispensable oceanic foundation and the free progression of products.

Robbery, however frequently romanticized in verifiable stories, stays a contemporary test for the oceanic commercial center. While robbery has been to a great extent stifled in specific locales through global maritime endeavors, it keeps on representing a danger in others, especially off the shore of Somalia and in the Bay of Guinea. The battle against robbery includes a mix of maritime watches, global co-operation, and endeavors to address the underlying drivers of theft, like destitution and political precariousness.

The lawful and administrative system administering the sea commercial center is intricate and complex. Worldwide shows, like the Unified Countries Show on the Law of the Ocean (UNCLOS), give a system to the expectations of states in sea spaces. Public wards, port guidelines, ecological norms, and wellbeing conventions further add to the complicated snare of guidelines that oversee sea exercises. Consistence with these guidelines is fundamental for guaranteeing the wellbeing of sea tasks, safeguarding the marine climate, and advancing fair and evenhanded exchange rehearses.

The oceanic commercial center is likewise a basic part of the worldwide store network, and interruptions can have extensive outcomes. The Coronavirus pandemic, for instance, uncovered weaknesses in the oceanic production network as ports confronted terminations, team changes became testing, and interest for specific merchandise varied unusually. Such disturbances highlight the requirement for strength and flexibility in the sea business, provoking a reassessment of store network systems and hazard the executives rehearses.

The job of ports in the oceanic commercial center couldn't possibly be more significant. Ports act as key points of interaction among land and ocean, working with the exchange of freight, travelers, and data. The productivity and limit of ports are urgent elements in deciding the general adequacy of the oceanic store network.

Modernizing port framework, streamlining freight taking care of cycles, and consolidating computerized advancements are fundamental stages in improving the seriousness of ports in the worldwide commercial center.

The sea commercial center isn't insusceptible to the continuous advanced change that is reshaping businesses across the globe. From blockchain innovation to the Web of Things (IoT), advanced developments are finding applications in the sea area that smooth out activities, upgrade straightforwardness, and work on in general proficiency. The utilization of computerized stages for freight following, electronic documentation, and continuous correspondence between partners is turning out to be progressively predominant, introducing another period of network and information driven independent direction.

Online protection has arisen as a basic worry in the oceanic business as it embraces digitalization. The interconnected idea of sea frameworks, including route, correspondence, and freight the executives, conveys them powerless against digital intimidations. Guaranteeing the online protection of sea foundation is basic for defending against likely disturbances, unapproved access, and information penetrates that could think twice about wellbeing and security of oceanic tasks.

The sea commercial center is a huge and perplexing biological system, enveloping a different exhibit of partners, each assuming an exceptional part in the working of the worldwide oceanic organization. Shipowners, delivering organizations, port administrators, oceanic specialists, and global associations work together and contend inside this complicated climate. Market elements, monetary patterns, and international occasions all impact the fortunes of the oceanic business, expecting partners to explore an ocean of vulnerabilities with strength and key premonition.

The human component stays a fundamental calculate the sea commercial center. Gifted sailors, including commanders, officials, specialists, and group individuals, structure the foundation of oceanic tasks. Their ability, experience, and commitment are urgent for guaranteeing the protected and effective development of vessels across the oceans. Be that as it may, the prosperity of sailors has been a developing worry, with issues like broadened agreements, weakness, and psychological well-being difficulties drawing consideration and inciting calls for worked on working circumstances.

The sea commercial center is additionally dependent upon monetary powers that shape worldwide exchange and impact delivering designs. Financial slumps, variances in item costs, and changes in buyer request all have expanding influences on the oceanic business. The capacity of the oceanic area to adjust to changing financial circumstances, improve because of market requests, and differentiate its administrations is fundamental for its proceeded with development and flexibility.

2.1 Exploration of diverse industries thriving in coastal regions

Waterfront locales, with their remarkable mix of regular assets, vital area, and admittance to sea shipping lanes, act as unique center points for a different cluster of businesses. From fisheries and the travel industry to energy creation and assembling, these districts assume a vital part in the monetary scene, contributing essentially to neighborhood and worldwide success. The investigation of assorted enterprises flourishing in seaside regions uncovers the unpredictable exchange between natural elements, financial exercises, and the reasonable improvement of these imperative locales.

The fishing business remains as one of the most seasoned and most customary areas in waterfront locales, depending on the plentiful marine assets that portray these regions. Beach front networks all over the planet participate in different types of fishing, going from limited scope high quality tasks to huge scope business undertakings. Fisheries contribute not exclusively to nearby economies yet in addition to worldwide food security, as fish stays a basic protein hotspot for a critical piece of the total populace. Supportable administration practices and protection endeavors are fundamental to guarantee the drawn out reasonability of fisheries and the conservation of marine environments.

Portraits Of Coastal Commerce

The travel industry, one more foundation of monetary action in beach front districts, flourishes with the regular excellence and sporting open doors that these regions offer. Ocean side hotels, beach front towns, and picturesque scenes draw in large number of sightseers every year, animating nearby economies and giving business open doors. Be that as it may, the quick development of waterfront the travel industry presents difficulties connected with natural protection, framework advancement, and the conservation of social legacy. Finding some kind of harmony between the travel industry driven monetary development and the security of waterfront environments is a basic thought for supportable turn of events.

The energy area has progressively tracked down a traction in beach front districts, saddling the force of regular assets like breeze, waves, and tides. Waterfront regions give ideal circumstances to the organization of environmentally friendly power advances, including seaward wind ranches and flowing energy establishments. These ventures not just add to the progress to a cleaner energy blend yet additionally set out positions and monetary open doors in waterfront networks. Be that as it may, the improvement of waterfront energy framework requires cautious wanting to moderate expected ecological effects and address concerns connected with visual style, route, and marine life.

Producing enterprises likewise flourish in waterfront areas, utilizing the benefits of oceanic transportation and admittance to natural substances. Ports and modern zones along shores work with the import of unrefined substances and the commodity of completed merchandise, making financial center points that drive territorial turn of events.

Shipbuilding, synthetic handling, and weighty assembling are among the areas that track down a characteristic home in beach front regions. Notwithstanding, the natural impression of modern exercises requires compelling ecological administration procedures to forestall contamination and safeguard waterfront biological systems.

Hydroponics, the development of sea-going creatures, has arisen as a critical industry in beach front locales, adding to food creation and financial development. Fish and shellfish cultivating tasks exploit the supplement rich waters close to shores to develop an assortment of fish items. While hydroponics presents open doors for broadening and expanded food creation, it additionally raises worries about water quality, illness the board, and the likely effects on wild fisheries. Reasonable practices and dependable hydroponics the executives are critical for limiting the ecological impression of this developing industry.

Delivery and sea transport structure the foundation of beach front economies, associating areas and working with worldwide exchange. Ports, filling in as pivotal hubs in the sea store network, handle the parcel of merchandise, work with worldwide exchange, and contribute altogether to financial turn of events. The proficiency and limit of ports assume an unequivocal part in the seriousness of waterfront districts in the worldwide commercial center. As exchange volumes keep on developing, the extension and modernization of port foundation become basic for supporting monetary development and keeping a consistent progression of merchandise.

Waterfront districts are much of the time wealthy in biodiversity and regular assets, making them ideal areas for the extraction of minerals and unrefined substances. Mining exercises, including sand extraction, mineral mining, and oil and gas investigation, add to the monetary improvement of waterfront regions. Notwithstanding, the natural effect of these exercises, like living space disturbance and contamination, requires rigid administrative structures and reasonable practices to guarantee the dependable extraction of assets without compromising the honesty of beach front environments.

Notwithstanding customary businesses, beach front districts are becoming center points for advancement and innovation improvement. Research establishments, marine labs, and innovation organizations are progressively attracted to beach front regions to investigate the huge capability of marine assets and environments. Progresses in marine biotechnology, oceanography, and natural observing contribute not exclusively to logical information yet additionally to the advancement of new enterprises and advancements with applications going from drugs to environmentally friendly power.

Sustainable power projects, especially seaward wind ranches, are changing waterfront locales into power age centers. The nearness of these areas to solid and steady breezes makes them ideal for saddling wind energy to satisfy developing power need.

The improvement of seaward wind foundation requires coordinated effort between the energy area, natural associations, and neighborhood networks to address concerns connected with visual effect, marine life, and expected clashes with other sea utilizes.

Beach front locales likewise assume a critical part in a fiasco versatility and reaction, given their weakness to cataclysmic events like typhoons, waves, and tempest floods. Framework advancement, early admonition frameworks, and local area readiness are fundamental parts of calamity risk decrease here. Beach front administration systems that coordinate ecological protection, feasible turn of events, and calamity flexibility are basic for guaranteeing the security and prosperity of waterfront networks notwithstanding expanding environment related difficulties.

As seaside locales proceed to develop and adjust to evolving financial, ecological, and social elements, the idea of blue economy acquires unmistakable quality. The blue economy accentuates the practical utilization of marine assets for financial development, work creation, and ecological preservation. This comprehensive methodology thinks about the interconnectedness of different areas, including fisheries, the travel industry, energy, and examination, and looks to offset financial improvement with the security of marine biological systems.

Challenges, in any case, have large amounts of the journey for practical improvement in waterfront locales. Environmental change, ocean level ascent, overfishing, contamination, and territory debasement present critical dangers to the sensitive equilibrium of waterfront biological systems. Coordinated waterfront the board moves toward that consider the aggregate effects of human exercises and regular cycles are urgent for tending to these difficulties. Neighborhood and worldwide joint effort, informed by logical exploration and local area commitment, is fundamental for encouraging strength and guaranteeing the economical fate of seaside districts.

All in all, the investigation of different enterprises flourishing in waterfront districts divulges an embroidery of monetary exercises, each impacted by the special qualities of these unique regions. From the conventional quests for fishing and the travel industry to the inventive domains of sustainable power and innovation improvement, beach front locales typify a nexus of chances and difficulties. Economical improvement rehearses, educated by an all encompassing comprehension regarding the interconnectedness of beach front biological systems and human exercises, are basic for guaranteeing the life span and essentialness of these imperative locales notwithstanding a quickly influencing world.

2.2 Successful coastal businesses and their impact on local economies

Beach front organizations, with their vicinity to the ocean and admittance to sea shipping lanes, assume a urgent part in forming neighborhood economies and adding to the general thriving of waterfront networks. These ventures length many businesses, each utilizing the interesting benefits presented by seaside areas. Effective seaside organizations animate monetary development as well as set out work open doors, drive advancement, and cultivate local area improvement. An investigation of these undertakings and their effect on nearby economies gives understanding into the dynamic and interconnected nature of seaside business environments.

Fisheries and Hydroponics:

The fishing business, well established in waterfront customs, stays a foundation of numerous beach front economies. Fruitful fisheries, whether limited scope distinctive tasks or enormous business undertakings, contribute fundamentally to nearby economies by giving work and providing fish to provincial and worldwide business sectors. The monetary effect of fisheries stretches out past direct catch and deals, affecting related enterprises like handling, circulation, and retail. Besides, feasible fishing rehearses are fundamental for the drawn out reasonability of fisheries and the protection of marine biological systems, guaranteeing a proceeded with type of revenue and food for seaside networks.

Notwithstanding conventional fisheries, hydroponics has arisen as a flourishing waterfront business. Fish and shellfish cultivating tasks exploit waterfront waters to develop an assortment of fish items. Effective hydroponics undertakings improve food creation as well as add to financial expansion and occupation creation in beach front regions. Nonetheless, maintainable practices and mindful administration are critical to relieve likely natural effects and guarantee the biological honesty of waterfront waters.

The travel industry and Accommodation:

Seaside locales, with their picturesque scenes, immaculate sea shores, and sporting open doors, draw in great many sightseers every year. The travel industry and cordiality area, incorporating ocean side retreats, lodgings, cafés, and different sporting exercises, comprises a critical part of waterfront organizations. Effective the travel industry undertakings add to the nearby economy by producing income, making position, and advancing social trade. The expanding influence stretches out to supporting nearby craftsmans, visit administrators, and transportation administrations.

The effect of the travel industry on neighborhood economies, nonetheless, requires cautious administration to address potential difficulties like ecological corruption, packing, and the safeguarding of social legacy. Maintainable the travel industry rehearses, local area commitment, and dependable advancement are critical for guaranteeing that the monetary advantages of the travel industry line up with the drawn out prosperity of waterfront networks.

Ports and Delivery:

Seaside regions frequently have significant ports, filling in as imperative entryways for worldwide exchange. Ports, with their foundation for freight taking care of, stockpiling, and transportation, are central participants in the worldwide production network. Effective port tasks contribute essentially to the monetary advancement of waterfront districts by working with the development of merchandise, cultivating exchange, and setting out business open doors. The proficiency and intensity of ports straightforwardly influence the generally speaking monetary presentation of waterfront regions, impacting businesses going from assembling to farming.

Delivering, intently attached to port exercises, likewise assumes an essential part in beach front economies. Effective delivery organizations interface waterfront districts to worldwide business sectors, moving merchandise and natural substances across oceans and seas. The sea exchange worked with by delivery adds to monetary development, work creation, and the foundation of key associations between waterfront networks and the more extensive worldwide economy.

Sustainable power:

Beach front regions, with their closeness to solid and reliable breezes, sea flows, and flowing streams, give ideal circumstances to the improvement of sustainable power projects. Seaward wind ranches, flowing energy establishments, and wave energy converters add to the change to a cleaner and more feasible energy blend. Fruitful environmentally friendly power organizations in beach front areas produce clean power as well as animate monetary development by making position and drawing in speculations.

Notwithstanding, the improvement of sustainable power foundation requires cautious thought of ecological effects, possible contentions with other sea uses, and local area commitment. Adjusting the monetary advantages of sustainable power with the conservation of marine environments is fundamental for guaranteeing the drawn out progress and acknowledgment of these tasks in beach front networks.

Oceanic Innovation and Advancement:

Seaside locales, frequently center points of oceanic action, draw in organizations zeroed in on mechanical advancement and exploration. Organizations associated with sea innovation foster high level route frameworks, correspondence advancements, and computerized arrangements that upgrade the proficiency and security of sea tasks. Effective oceanic innovation organizations contribute not exclusively to the financial improvement of beach front regions yet in addition to the worldwide sea industry's advancement.

Research foundations, marine labs, and innovation new businesses are attracted to waterfront locales to investigate the huge capability of marine assets and biological systems. Progresses in marine biotechnology, oceanography, and ecological observing have applications going from drugs to sustainable power.

The fruitful cooperation between the scholarly world, industry, and neighborhood networks encourages development and drives monetary enhancement in beach front locales.

Land and Beach front Turn of events:

Beach front land improvement, incorporating private, business, and the travel industry related projects, is a huge supporter of neighborhood economies. Fruitful land adventures in waterfront regions give lodging and framework as well as animate financial action through development, accommodation administrations, and retail. Notwithstanding, beach front advancement raises worries about ecological preservation, environment assurance, and the potential for expanded weakness to catastrophic events.

Adjusting the interest for seaside land with reasonable improvement rehearses is fundamental for saving the regular magnificence and biological respectability of beach front locales. Capable land-use arranging, adherence to construction laws, and local area commitment are critical components in guaranteeing that land improvement contributes emphatically to neighborhood economies without compromising the climate.

Journey Industry:

The journey business, based on beach front and port exercises, is a critical player in the worldwide travel area. Journey lines work vessels that cross the world's seas, giving travelers a novel travel experience that incorporates visits to beach front objections. Fruitful voyage organizations add to neighborhood economies by carrying vacationers to beach front locales, invigorating retail, neighborliness, and visit administrations.

Nonetheless, the journey business likewise faces difficulties connected with natural maintainability, especially concerning air and water contamination, squander the executives, and the effect on nearby environments. Economical practices, interests in green advancements, and joint effort with waterfront networks are fundamental for guaranteeing that the journey business keeps on contributing emphatically to nearby economies while limiting its ecological impression.

Debacle Strength and Seaside Administrations:

Waterfront locales are vulnerable to catastrophic events like typhoons, tidal waves, and tempest floods. Organizations that give catastrophe versatility administrations, including early admonition frameworks, foundation improvement, and crisis reaction, assume a urgent part in shielding seaside networks. Fruitful endeavors in this area add to the security and prosperity of occupants, as well as the protection of basic framework.

Beach front administrations additionally incorporate exercises connected with natural preservation, territory rebuilding, and economical asset the board. Organizations participated in these administrations add to the drawn out soundness of beach front environments, supporting biodiversity and advancing a decent concurrence between human exercises and nature.

All in all, fruitful beach front organizations are basic to the monetary energy and flexibility of seaside districts. From conventional areas like fisheries and the travel industry to arising ventures, for example, sustainable power and sea innovation, these endeavors add to work creation, financial development, and local area advancement. The manageability of beach front organizations requires an all encompassing methodology that thinks about natural preservation, local area commitment, and mindful strategic policies. As beach front locales keep on developing despite worldwide difficulties, fruitful organizations assume a significant part in molding a future where financial success remains closely connected with ecological stewardship and local area prosperity.

2.3 Analysis of how geographical factors influence the types of commerce in different coastal areas

Geological elements assume a crucial part in molding the sorts of business that flourish in various beach front regions all over the planet. From the actual attributes of shorelines to the climatic circumstances and normal assets accessible, the geological setting significantly impacts the financial exercises that can be supported in these areas. An examination of how geological variables add to the variety of trade in different beach front regions uncovers the mind boggling exchange among nature and financial turn of events.

1. **Actual Geology:**

    The actual highlights of shorelines essentially influence the kinds of trade that can be laid out in waterfront regions. The presence of profound normal harbors and shielded inlets works with sea exercises, empowering the improvement of fruitful port urban areas and transportation centers. For instance, the deepwater ports of Rotterdam in the Netherlands and Singapore's essential area along significant transportation courses have added to the development of these areas as worldwide sea and exchanging focuses.

Conversely, rough shores or shallow waters might restrict the improvement of huge ports and transportation exercises however might be reasonable for enterprises like fisheries and hydroponics. Seaside regions with broad wetlands or swamps might be helpful for exercises like salt creation, while those with sandy sea shores might draw in the travel industry and sporting enterprises.

2. **Environment and Weather conditions:**

   Environment and weather conditions impact the sorts of business that can flourish in waterfront regions. Districts with heat and humidities might be more reasonable for the travel industry and farming, enabled the enticement for develop various harvests. Waterfront regions subject to visit tempests or tropical storms might confront difficulties in laying out and keeping up with framework, impacting the sorts of organizations that can work effectively.

   For example, the Caribbean's warm environment and immaculate sea shores make it a well known objective for the travel industry, while districts along the Bay of Mexico, regardless of confronting storm gambles, are basic for the oil and gas industry. The occasional varieties in environment, like storms in pieces of Southeast Asia, additionally influence the timing and nature of monetary exercises, affecting business in these beach front regions.

3. **Normal Assets:**

   The accessibility of normal assets in beach front regions shapes the sorts of business that can prosper. Fisheries and hydroponics are pervasive in regions wealthy in marine assets, giving a wellspring of occupation to waterfront networks. The extraction of minerals, including oil and gas, frequently happens in waterfront districts with bountiful seaward saves.

   For instance, the North Ocean's rich fishing grounds support a vigorous fisheries industry, while the North Ocean's oil and gas holds have prompted the improvement of a flourishing energy area. Likewise, waterfront regions with rich soils might be helpful for horticulture, with crops going from rice in Southeast Asia to wine creation in Mediterranean districts.

4. **Environment Variety:**

   The variety of waterfront environments impacts the sorts of trade that can be supported while likewise presenting contemplations for feasible turn of events. Waterfront wetlands, mangroves, and estuaries are basic living spaces that help biodiversity, going about as nurseries for fish and giving security from storm floods. Offsetting financial exercises with the protection of these biological systems is fundamental for long haul manageability.

   For example, the Florida Everglades in the US support the travel industry, fisheries, and agribusiness, however their safeguarding is urgent for keeping up with the strength of the district's one of a kind environment. Mangrove timberlands in beach front areas of Southeast Asia add to fisheries and safeguard against disintegration, featuring the significance of protection in advancing manageable business.

5. **Availability and Network:**

   Geological factors, for example, closeness to significant shipping lanes and transportation foundation impact the availability and network of seaside regions. Ports situated along key oceanic courses become significant center points for worldwide exchange, drawing in organizations engaged with transportation, coordinated operations, and exchange related administrations.

   The Suez Channel's essential area associating the Mediterranean Ocean to the Red Ocean has made the seaside regions encompassing it indispensable for worldwide exchange.

   Likewise, the Panama Trench's part in associating the Atlantic and Pacific Seas has molded the business and improvement of beach front regions in Focal America. The simplicity of transportation and network to worldwide business sectors can upgrade the seriousness of organizations in these waterfront locales.

6. **Geography and Land Use:**

   The geography of waterfront regions, including the accessibility of level land and appropriate structure locales, impacts the kinds of business that can be laid out. Level seaside fields might be helpful for the advancement of ports, modern zones, and metropolitan regions. Interestingly, regions with steep bluffs or rough territory might restrict improvement choices and favor enterprises that require less framework.

   For example, the modern advancement of seaside regions in the Pearl Waterway Delta in China has been worked with by the level geology, making it a financial force to be reckoned with flourishing assembling and exchange exercises. Beach front regions with normal harbors and protected inlets might energize the foundation of marinas and waterfront advancements, adding to the travel industry and sporting trade.

7. **Social and Authentic Setting:**

   Social and verifiable factors likewise assume a huge part in forming the kinds of trade in beach front regions. Customary practices, social legacy, and verifiable associations with the ocean impact financial exercises. Fishing people group with a well established oceanic practice might keep on flourishing with fisheries, while verifiable port urban communities might have broadened economies driven in terms of professional career and business.

   The Mediterranean district, with its rich history of marine civic establishments, has impacted the improvement of seaside regions with an emphasis on the travel industry, horticulture, and sea exchange. Social contemplations additionally influence the travel industry, as seaside regions with authentic tourist spots, social celebrations, and novel customs might draw in guests looking for improving encounters.

8. **Natural Weakness and Versatility:**

   Beach front regions are frequently powerless against ecological difficulties, for example, rising ocean levels, disintegration, and tempest floods. Geological elements that add to natural weakness impact the sorts of organizations that can work reasonably. Organizations associated with calamity flexibility, seaside assurance, and feasible land utilize become critical for alleviating ecological dangers.

   For instance, the Netherlands, with a huge piece of its property beneath ocean level, has created inventive water the board techniques and innovations. The Dutch skill in beach front designing has made them worldwide innovators in giving answers for overseeing water levels and safeguarding seaside regions from flooding.

9. **Administrative and Administration Systems:**

   The administrative and administration systems set up in seaside regions impact the sorts of business that can be laid out and supported. Drafting guidelines, natural security regulations, and land-use arranging influence the improvement of ventures and foundation along shores. Feasible practices and adherence to administrative necessities become fundamental for organizations looking to work in seaside regions.

   For example, waterfront regions in Scandinavia have severe natural guidelines, affecting enterprises to take on feasible practices. The administration systems likewise assume a part in overseeing clashes between various monetary exercises, for example, adjusting the interests of fisheries with those of sustainable power projects.

10. **Worldwide Financial Patterns:**

Topographical variables in waterfront regions are likewise affected by more extensive worldwide financial patterns. The interest for specific products, changes in buyer inclinations, and headways in innovation can affect the sorts of trade that flourish in waterfront locales. For instance, the rising spotlight on environmentally friendly power has prompted the improvement of seaward wind ranches in waterfront regions, adding to the development of the green economy.

Worldwide monetary patterns, like the ascent of web based business and changes in assembling designs, can impact the strategies and transportation areas in beach front districts. The flexibility of waterfront organizations to these worldwide patterns is pivotal for supported development and seriousness.

Trade in various seaside regions is formed by a horde of elements, going from geological and ecological circumstances to verifiable, social, and financial impacts. The unique exchange of these components makes assorted monetary scenes along shores around the world. Dissecting trade in various beach front regions gives experiences into the exceptional difficulties and amazing open doors that organizations face, mirroring the many-sided connection among topography and monetary action.

1. **North Ocean Locale:**

    The North Ocean locale, enveloping nations like the Netherlands, Germany, and the Unified Realm, flaunts a strong sea economy well established in its topographical benefits. The broad shore, regular harbors, and traversable streams have cultivated a flourishing transportation and coordinated operations area. Significant ports like Rotterdam, one of the biggest on the planet, work with the parcel of merchandise, making the locale a critical center point for worldwide exchange.

    Notwithstanding oceanic business, the North Ocean locale is described by major areas of strength for an on seaward energy. Immense oil and gas saves underneath the North Ocean have driven the improvement of a refined energy industry, with seaward penetrating stages and extraction tasks contributing fundamentally to the local economy. The Netherlands, specifically, has arisen as a forerunner in seaward wind energy, saddling serious areas of strength for the of the North Ocean to produce feasible power.

    Fisheries likewise assume a crucial part in the North Ocean's beach front business. The rich fishing grounds support a different scope of animal types, supporting nearby fishing networks and adding to the more extensive European fish market. The multi-layered nature of trade in the North Ocean area highlights the versatility of waterfront economies to use assorted assets for supported development.

2. **Caribbean Islands:**

    The Caribbean islands, with their immaculate sea shores and heat and humidities, have developed an energetic the travel industry that frames the foundation of waterfront business. Nations like the Bahamas, Jamaica, and the Dominican Republic depend intensely on the travel industry related exercises, including resorts, journey transport objections, and sporting administrations. The normal excellence of the Caribbean, combined with its warm environment, makes it a sought-after objective for explorers from around the world.

    The travel industry in the Caribbean not just adds to neighborhood economies through friendliness benefits yet additionally animates subordinate businesses like painstaking work, social encounters, and water-based exercises. The district's geological elements, including coral reefs and marine biodiversity, give exceptional attractions to jumpers and eco-travelers. Be that as it may, the weakness of these islands to tropical storms and environmental change highlights the requirement for reasonable the travel industry practices and debacle flexibility measures.

Portraits Of Coastal Commerce 39

Past the travel industry, some Caribbean countries participate in fisheries, especially limited scope activities focusing on neighborhood markets. The development of tropical harvests, like bananas and sugarcane, additionally adds to the waterfront economy. The Caribbean represents how topographical traits, for this situation, regular magnificence and heat and humidity, can shape a prevalently the travel industry driven waterfront business.

3. **Inlet of Guinea:**

The Inlet of Guinea, on the west shore of Africa, is portrayed by different seaside economies impacted by variables like oil and gas extraction, fisheries, and oceanic exchange. Nations like Nigeria, Tropical Guinea, and Ghana have critical oil holds, prompting the improvement of a flourishing oil and gas area along their shores. The extraction, handling, and product of oil contribute considerably to government incomes and unfamiliar trade profit.

Fisheries in the Bay of Guinea are likewise essential for seaside trade, giving business and food to nearby networks. Nonetheless, difficulties, for example, overfishing and unlawful, unreported, and unregulated (IUU) fishing present dangers to the manageability of these assets. The geological variety of the Inlet of Guinea, with its mangroves, estuaries, and tidal ponds, adds to the rich marine biodiversity that upholds fisheries.

Sea exchange is worked with by significant ports in the area, like Lagos in Nigeria and Tema in Ghana. The Bay of Guinea's essential area along worldwide delivery courses highlights its significance for global exchange. Notwithstanding the monetary potential, issues of robbery and security worries in certain region of the Bay feature the mind boggling elements that impact beach front trade.

4. **Southeast Asia:**

Southeast Asia, with its perplexing organization of shores and archipelagos, is home to assorted beach front economies molded by geological elements. Nations like Indonesia, Thailand, and Vietnam display a scope of business impacted by fisheries, hydroponics, the travel industry, and oceanic exchange.

The district's broad coral reefs and marine biodiversity support dynamic fisheries that contribute fundamentally to neighborhood occupations and territorial products. Moreover, hydroponics, especially shrimp cultivating, has turned into a significant industry in nations like Vietnam and Thailand. The geological overflow of waterfront regions with reasonable circumstances for hydroponics has filled the development of this area.

The travel industry is a vital driver of waterfront business in Southeast Asia, with nations like Thailand and the Philippines drawing in huge number of guests yearly. The beautiful sea shores, social legacy locales, and various marine conditions make these beach front locations well known among worldwide and homegrown vacationers. Nonetheless, the quick development of the travel industry likewise raises worries about ecological corruption and the conservation of social personalities.

Oceanic exchange is worked with by significant ports in the district, for example, Singapore, which has arisen as a worldwide delivery and planned operations center. The essential area of Southeast Asia along significant sea courses upgrades its job in global exchange, adding to the financial dynamism of waterfront regions.

5. **Cold District:**

The Cold district, described by its frigid scenes and testing ecological circumstances, is encountering advancing examples of business impacted by elements, for example, environmental change, asset extraction, and transportation courses. Softening ice has opened up new open doors for oceanic exercises, including transportation and asset investigation.

The Northern Ocean Course, which interfaces Europe and Asia along the Icy coast, has acquired consideration as a likely easy route for delivery, essentially diminishing travel times. As ice withdraws, the Cold has become progressively available for asset extraction, including oil, gas, and minerals. Beach front regions in Russia, Canada, and Scandinavia are seeing the improvement of enterprises connected with Cold transportation and asset abuse.

Fisheries, especially those focusing on chilly water species, are likewise present in the Icy district, adding to nearby economies. In any case, the fragile Cold environments and the effect of environmental change raise worries about the manageability of these exercises. The advancing elements of trade in the Cold highlight the mind boggling transaction between geological changes and financial open doors.

6. **Mediterranean District:**

The Mediterranean district, encompassed by different shores and rich verifiable heritages, has various waterfront economies affected by the travel industry, fisheries, horticulture, and sea exchange. Nations like Italy, Greece, and Spain benefit from their authentic port urban areas, social legacy, and beautiful scenes.

The travel industry assumes a focal part in the seaside trade of the Mediterranean, with a great many guests drawn to the district's notable locales, delightful sea shores, and energetic waterfront towns. The interest for social encounters, culinary pleasures, and sporting exercises upholds a great many organizations, including lodgings, cafés, and visit administrations.

Fisheries add to the beach front economy, with the Mediterranean Ocean being home to different financially significant species. Notwithstanding, overfishing and ecological debasement present difficulties to the maintainability of fisheries. Farming, including the development of olive forests and grape plantations, is predominant in seaside regions, adding to both nearby and worldwide business sectors.

Sea exchange is worked with by significant ports in the Mediterranean, like the Port of Piraeus in Greece and the Port of Valencia in Spain. The authentic significance of these ports, combined with their essential areas, improves the locale's job in global exchange. The Mediterranean embodies how geological and authentic elements cross to shape different beach front economies.

7. **Pacific Islands:**

   The Pacific Islands, scattered across huge sea spans, display waterfront economies affected by variables like fisheries, the travel industry, and social practices. Nations like Fiji, Samoa, and the Cook Islands depend on a blend of conventional exercises and present day businesses to support their seaside trade.

   Fisheries are a huge part of the Pacific Islands' economies, giving food security and pay to neighborhood networks. Conventional fishing rehearses, for example, utilizing outrigger kayaks and handlines, coincide with present day business fishing activities. Notwithstanding, issues, for example, overfishing and the effect of environmental change on marine biological systems present difficulties to the maintainability of fisheries.

   The travel industry, driven by the charm of tropical heavens and interesting social encounters, adds to the seaside economies of Pacific Islands. The interest for eco-accommodating and socially vivid the travel industry encounters has prompted the advancement of manageable the travel industry rehearses. Nonetheless, the weakness of these islands to environmental change, including rising ocean levels and outrageous climate occasions, requires cautious administration of the travel industry related exercises.

8. **East Bank of the US:**

The East Bank of the US, extending from Maine to Florida, has a different scope of waterfront economies impacted by elements like oceanic exchange, fisheries, the travel industry, and land improvement. Significant urban communities like New York, Miami, and Boston have clamoring ports that work with global exchange, making the East Coast an imperative player in the nation's economy.

Sea exchange, upheld by significant ports like the Port of New York and New Jersey, associates the East Coast to worldwide business sectors. The essential area of these ports upgrades the locale's seriousness in worldwide exchange, with an emphasis on holder delivery, planned operations, and dispersion.

Fisheries, albeit affected by overfishing and ecological changes, stay significant for the seaside economies of states like Maine and Massachusetts. The rich marine biological systems off the East Coast support various economically significant species, adding to the fish business.

The travel industry assumes a huge part along the East Coast, with famous locations, for example, Cape Cod, Miami Ocean side, and the External Banks drawing in guests looking for ocean side get-aways, social encounters, and verifiable locales.

The land area, driven by beach front turn of events and waterfront properties, additionally adds to the locale's monetary elements.

Chapter 3

Tides of Innovation

In the tremendous scope of mankind's set of experiences, the tides of development have ebbed and streamed, molding the course of civic establishments and making a permanent imprint on the embroidered artwork of progress. From the unassuming starting points of the wheel to the perplexing calculations of man-made consciousness, advancement has been the main impetus behind humankind's rising. A power rises above lines, societies, and ages, winding around a story of creativity and flexibility.

The earliest reverberates of advancement can be followed back to the beginning of civilization. In the Ripe Bow, where the support of human development flourished, the wheel arose as an extraordinary creation. Its effortlessness misrepresented its significant effect on transportation and exchange, proclaiming another period of versatility. With the wheel, people could navigate distances with more noteworthy productivity, working with the trading of merchandise and thoughts across thriving networks.

As social orders advanced, so did their techniques for correspondence. The composed word, a development in itself, turned into a foundation of human advancement. Old civilizations like Mesopotamia and Egypt scratched their accounts onto earth tablets and papyrus scrolls, making a put down account that rose above the verbally expressed word. This advancement saved information as well as laid the basis for the spread of thoughts across ages.

The tides of advancement kept on flooding through the ages, each wave delivering new innovations and perspective changes. The Renaissance, a social and scholarly recovery in Europe during the fourteenth to seventeenth hundreds of years, saw a blast of imagination in human expression and sciences. Advancements like the print machine, credited to Johannes Gutenberg, reformed the spread of data, making books more open and democratizing information.

The Modern Transformation, a seismic change in the eighteenth and nineteenth hundreds of years, denoted the progress from agrarian economies to industrialized social orders. Steam motors, automated creation, and the tackling of power changed the scene of work and industry. The constant walk of development pushed humankind into the cutting edge period, making way for phenomenal headways.

In the twentieth hundred years, the speed of advancement advanced with stunning rate. The appearance of the vehicle, the plane, and media communications introduced a time of worldwide network. The world, once tremendous and far off, turned out to be more interconnected than any time in recent memory. Notwithstanding, the century likewise demonstrated the veracity of the disastrous force of development, as two universal conflicts displayed the clouded side of innovative advancement.

The post-war time frame delivered another flood of advancement, filled by the race for space investigation and the development of figuring innovations. The moon arrival in 1969 was a demonstration of human desire and the steady quest for the unexplored world. In the mean time, the improvement of PCs and the introduction of the web established the groundwork for the Data Age, changing how individuals conveyed, worked, and lived.

The late twentieth 100 years and mid 21st century saw the ascent of Silicon Valley and the advanced insurgency. Advancements in individualized computing, programming improvement, and the web re-imagined the manner in which individuals collaborated with data. The approach of online entertainment stages additionally sped up the trading of thoughts, making virtual networks that rose above geological limits.

As the 21st century unfurled, the tides of advancement arrived at phenomenal levels. The combination of innovations, like man-made reasoning, biotechnology, and sustainable power, vowed to reshape the actual texture of human life.

The Fourth Modern Unrest, portrayed by the combination of the physical, computerized, and organic domains, proclaimed another period of conceivable outcomes and difficulties.

Computerized reasoning, specifically, arose as a groundbreaking power, with the possibility to reform businesses going from medical care to fund. AI calculations, fit for handling tremendous measures of information, guaranteed experiences and efficiencies beforehand unbelievable. Be that as it may, this mechanical jump additionally raised moral worries about security, predisposition, and the effect on business.

Biotechnology, one more boondocks of advancement, opened the mysteries of the human genome and opened new wildernesses in medication. CRISPR-Cas9, a progressive quality altering innovation, offered the possibility of killing hereditary illnesses and redoing the human genome. However, the moral ramifications of playing with the very assembling blocks of life incited warmed discussions and calls for administrative oversight.

Environmentally friendly power advances, driven by the pressing need to address environmental change, looked to reclassify the worldwide energy scene. Sun based and wind power arose as reasonable options in contrast to customary petroleum products, promising a more maintainable future. Developments in energy capacity and dissemination expected to conquer the irregular idea of sustainable sources, preparing for a cleaner and greener planet.

The interconnectedness of development likewise led to new difficulties on a worldwide scale. Network protection turned into a basic worry as the world turned out to be progressively dependent on computerized foundation. The danger of digital assaults, information breaks, and the weaponization of data brought up issues about the strength of current cultures despite developing mechanical dangers.

The democratization of data, worked with by the web, had significant ramifications for administration and international relations. Social developments, filled by online stages, picked up phenomenal speed, testing laid out power designs and forming public talk. Legislatures wrestled with the ramifications of a carefully associated populace, exploring the scarce difference between opportunity of articulation and the requirement for guideline.

Amidst these extraordinary changes, the job of training developed to fulfill the needs of a quickly influencing world. Conventional models of learning were enhanced by online stages, intuitive advances, and versatile learning frameworks. The accentuation moved from repetition remembrance to decisive reasoning, innovativeness, and versatility, planning people for a dynamic and unsure future.

The crossing point of advancement and medical care guaranteed forward leaps in analysis, therapy, and avoidance. Accuracy medication, custom-made to individual hereditary profiles, held the possibility to upset clinical practices.

Telemedicine and wearable innovations empowered remote checking and customized care, rising above geological hindrances and expanding openness.

Space investigation, when the area of a limited handful countries, entered another time of joint effort and commercialization. Privately owned businesses, driven by visionaries like Elon Musk and Jeff Bezos, looked to make space travel more open and practical. The possibility of colonizing different planets and mining space rocks opened up new boondocks for human investigation and asset usage.

In the midst of the rushes of development, cultural mentalities toward innovation went through a significant shift. The idealistic dreams of a flawlessly interconnected world were tempered by worries about security, disparity, and the potentially negative results of quick mechanical progression. As advancements outperformed administrative systems, the requirement for moral rules and mindful improvement turned out to be progressively evident.

The monetary scene went through seismic movements as conventional ventures confronted interruption and new areas arose. The gig economy, controlled by computerized stages, reclassified the idea of work and business. Robotization and man-made reasoning, while at the same time promising proficiency gains, additionally raised worries about work uprooting and the requirement for reskilling in the labor force.

The worldwide scene of development was not without its international ramifications. The race for mechanical incomparability turned into a characterizing element of worldwide relations. Countries competed for strength in fields, for example, 5G innovation, quantum processing, and man-made consciousness, perceiving the essential significance of advancement in molding the future international request.

The difficulties presented by the tides of development required a reconsideration of cultural qualities and needs. The quest for financial development and mechanical headway should have been offset with contemplations of maintainability, morals, and social value. As the world wrestled with the ramifications of a hyper-associated and quickly developing future, the requirement for an aggregate vision and co-operative arrangements turned out to be progressively obvious.

3.1 Examination of technological advancements in coastal commerce

The assessment of mechanical progressions in beach front trade uncovers a powerful exchange among development and the oceanic business' development. Waterfront districts, with their essential importance for exchange and transportation, have been at the cutting edge of taking on and adjusting to mechanical changes that upgrade productivity, wellbeing, and manageability.

The origin of seaside business traces all the way back to antiquated developments, where marine networks participated in exchange along shores. Be that as it may, the coordination of innovation has significantly changed this well established practice. The appearance of route helps, for example, beacons, denoted an early mechanical step, offering sailors pivotal direction and lessening the dangers related with waterfront route. Over the long run, headways in route innovation have become progressively complex, consolidating GPS frameworks, radar, and sonar, furnishing vessels with ongoing information and improving navigational precision.

One of the crucial progressions in seaside trade has been the improvement of containerization. Normalized delivering compartments reformed freight taking care of, smoothing out the stacking and dumping processes at ports. This development sped up the speed of exchange as well as worked on the general proficiency of oceanic coordinated operations. The far reaching reception of containerization worked with the ascent of uber holder ships, fit for conveying monster measures of freight across seas. These mechanical jumps reshaped worldwide stock chains, with beach front ports becoming crucial hubs in the interconnected trap of global exchange.

Mechanization arose as a distinct advantage in waterfront trade, changing port tasks and freight taking care of. Mechanized compartment terminals influence mechanical technology and man-made brainpower to improve proficiency, diminish work costs, and limit human mistake. Robotized cranes, directed by cutting edge calculations, can definitively position compartments, improving extra room and facilitating the exchange of products among boats and storage spaces. This speeds up the freight taking care of interaction as well as adds to more secure and all the more naturally maintainable port tasks.

The incorporation of Web of Things (IoT) gadgets has additionally upgraded the proficiency and security of seaside business. Savvy sensors implanted in steel trailers, port foundation, and vessels empower constant checking of freight conditions, compartment status, and ecological elements. This availability works with proactive navigation, permitting partners to answer quickly to unexpected difficulties, for example, unfriendly atmospheric conditions or gear breakdowns. Also, IoT innovations add to the advancement of savvy ports, where information driven bits of knowledge are tackled to streamline traffic stream, diminish blockage, and improve generally port execution.

As of late, the sea business has seen the rise of blockchain innovation as a groundbreaking power in beach front trade. Blockchain, with its decentralized and alter safe record framework, addresses longstanding difficulties connected with straightforwardness, security, and detectability in sea exchanges. Shrewd agreements, controlled by blockchain, empower robotized and secure execution of arrangements between different partners in the store network. This lessens the gamble of extortion as well as facilitates the settlement cycle, smoothing out monetary exchanges in beach front trade.

The ascent of e-route has achieved a change in outlook in how vessels explore beach front waters. Electronic outline frameworks, combined with constant information from satellite route frameworks, furnish sailors with thorough and cutting-edge navigational data. High level e-route apparatuses coordinate climate information, traffic data, and crash aversion frameworks, improving situational mindfulness and alleviating the dangers related with beach front route. This innovative union cultivates more secure and more effective sea transport along shorelines.

In the domain of ecological manageability, the sea business has been under expanding strain to diminish its carbon impression. Waterfront business, being an essential part of worldwide transportation, has seen the turn of events and reception of eco-accommodating innovations. Developments in impetus frameworks, like the usage of condensed flammable gas (LNG) and crossover electric motors, expect to limit discharges and follow severe ecological guidelines. Moreover, the investigation of wind-help advances, similar to sails and rotor sails, looks to outfit environmentally friendly power for drive, further adjusting waterfront business to economical practices.

The idea of independent vessels has arisen as a wilderness in mechanical progressions for waterfront trade. While completely independent boats are still in the trial stage, the business imagines a future where vessels explore seaside waters without human mediation. Independent innovations, directed by man-made reasoning and AI calculations, can possibly improve wellbeing, streamline route courses, and lessen functional expenses. In any case, the far reaching reception of independent vessels raises complex difficulties connected with administrative structures, online protection, and the moral ramifications of automated oceanic tasks.

Beach front business is additionally seeing the incorporation of 5G innovation, opening additional opportunities for correspondence and information trade. High velocity and low-idleness availability given by 5G organizations empowers ongoing correspondence between vessels, ports, and coordinated factors partners. This availability is essential for the execution of remote checking, prescient upkeep, and the consistent trade of information that supports the effectiveness of beach front business. The time of 5G envoys another flood of chances for advancement in sea correspondence, changing how data is shared and used in beach front locales.

The assessment of mechanical progressions in waterfront trade would be fragmented without tending to the effect of environmental change and rising ocean levels. Beach front regions are especially defenseless against the outcomes of environmental change, presenting dangers to foundation, route courses, and port tasks. Mechanical developments zeroed in on environment flexibility, for example, high level climate expectation models, early admonition frameworks, and versatile foundation plans, are turning out to be progressively basic for guaranteeing the supportability of seaside business notwithstanding natural difficulties.

All in all, the assessment of mechanical progressions in beach front trade uncovers a story of development, variation, and change. From antiquated route helps to the time of independent vessels and 5G network, the oceanic business has ceaselessly embraced innovative advancement to explore the perplexing waters of worldwide exchange. As beach front areas develop in light of financial, ecological, and mechanical powers, the joining of trend setting innovations stays vital for molding the fate of seaside business. The continuous interaction among custom and development guarantees that waterfront areas keep on being dynamic centers of monetary movement, where the tides of innovation push oceanic enterprises toward new skylines.

3.2 Impact of digitalization and automation on shipping, logistics, and port operations

The effect of digitalization and robotization on delivery, strategies, and port tasks is a significant change reshaping the scene of worldwide exchange and sea ventures. The joining of computerized advances and mechanized frameworks has introduced a period of effectiveness, straightforwardness, and development, reforming how products are shipped, made due, and took care of in ports across the world.

Digitalization, as an expansive idea, envelops the reception of computerized innovations to smooth out processes, improve network, and upgrade information the board in the transportation and strategies areas. The utilization of computerized stages, information examination, and high level correspondence frameworks has become vital to the modernization of supply chains. Ongoing information trade, worked with by computerized stages, has made a more interconnected and dexterous environment, permitting partners to pursue informed choices and answer quickly to evolving conditions.

In the domain of transportation, the effect of digitalization is most clear in the reception of Electronic Information Trade (EDI) and computerized documentation. Customarily, transporting documentation included a huge number of paper-based processes, bringing about postponements, blunders, and failures. The execution of EDI empowers the electronic trade of delivery archives, like bills of filling and customs announcements, decreasing desk work, limiting mistakes, and speeding up the leeway cycle. This digitization of documentation works on functional productivity as well as adds to a more feasible and harmless to the ecosystem transporting industry by diminishing the dependence on paper.

Worldwide Situating Framework (GPS) innovation has been a distinct advantage in oceanic route, permitting vessels to decide their exact area and explore with phenomenal precision. GPS, joined with satellite correspondence frameworks, has upgraded the wellbeing and proficiency of transportation by giving constant data on vessel developments, atmospheric conditions, and expected risks. Vessel global positioning frameworks fueled by GPS have likewise assumed a urgent part in fighting robbery and guaranteeing the security of oceanic courses.

Robotization has arisen as an extraordinary power in the transportation business, rethinking the manners by which vessels are worked and made due. Robotized frameworks, for example, High level Route Frameworks and Crash Evasion Frameworks, influence man-made reasoning and sensor innovations to advance course arranging, screen vessel execution, and improve route wellbeing. These frameworks add to the counteraction of impacts, groundings, and other navigational occurrences, alleviating gambles and working on in general oceanic security.

The idea of independent boats addresses the zenith of mechanical headway in delivery. While completely independent vessels are still in the exploratory stage, the business imagines a future where boats explore the oceans without human mediation. Independent delivery depends on state of the art innovations like Man-made reasoning (simulated intelligence), AI, and sensor combination to empower vessels to go with complex navigational choices, stay away from hindrances, and answer changing ecological circumstances. The possible advantages of independent delivery incorporate expanded functional proficiency, decreased human blunder, and lower fuel utilization, adding to a more maintainable and practical sea industry.

In the space of coordinated operations, digitalization has achieved a change in perspective in production network the executives. The utilization of Transportation The board Frameworks (TMS), Distribution center Administration Frameworks (WMS), and Venture Asset Arranging (ERP) programming has become typical, giving start to finish perceivability and command over the whole coordinated factors process. These computerized apparatuses empower proficient course arranging, stock administration, and request satisfaction, streamlining the progression of merchandise from makers to purchasers.

The Web of Things (IoT) assumes a crucial part in the computerized change of operations. IoT gadgets, for example, sensors and RFID labels, are utilized to track and screen the development of merchandise all through the inventory network. This ongoing perceivability empowers strategies suppliers to upgrade stock levels, limit lead times, and improve the general proficiency of coordinated factors activities. Furthermore, IoT-controlled resource global positioning frameworks add to the counteraction of burglary, misfortune, or harm to significant freight during transportation.

Blockchain innovation has arisen as a disruptor in the field of operations, presenting straightforwardness, security, and detectability to production network processes. Blockchain's decentralized and alter safe record framework works with trust and responsibility among partners in the production network. Brilliant agreements, empowered by blockchain, mechanize and get arrangements between parties, decreasing the requirement for delegates and smoothing out exchange processes. This not just improves the respectability of the inventory network yet in addition diminishes the gamble of extortion and blunders.

Digitalization has stretched out its compass to port tasks, where the streamlining of cycles through innovation has become basic for taking care of the developing volume of worldwide exchange. Port People group Frameworks (laptops) act as advanced stages that interface different partners, including transporting lines, port specialists, customs, and coordinated factors suppliers. Computers smooth out data trade, work with electronic documentation, and improve coordination among various substances associated with port tasks.

Robotized compartment terminals have turned into a sign of digitalization in port tasks. These terminals influence mechanical technology, Man-made consciousness (simulated intelligence), and information investigation to robotize the development of holders, from dumping and stacking to stacking onto vessels. Mechanized holder dealing with lessens dependence on physical work, increments functional effectiveness, and limits the gamble of mishaps. Terminal Working Frameworks (TOS) further add to the advanced change of ports by improving billet arranging, overseeing holder developments, and upgrading in general terminal efficiency.

The mix of information examination and prescient support has become instrumental in upgrading the presentation of port hardware and foundation. By examining information from sensors and observing frameworks, port administrators can recognize expected issues before they grow into exorbitant breakdowns. Prescient support decreases personal time as well as expands the life expectancy of basic port resources, adding to the manageability and unwavering quality of port tasks.

Computerized Twin innovation has gotten momentum in the oceanic business, offering a virtual portrayal of actual resources like vessels, ports, and planned operations offices. Computerized Twins empower port administrators to reproduce and break down different situations, streamline asset assignment, and recognize regions for development. This virtual demonstrating upgrades dynamic cycles, permitting partners to picture the effect of changes progressively and go with informed decisions that improve proficiency and asset use.

The groundbreaking effect of digitalization and robotization on delivery, strategies, and port activities reaches out past functional proficiency to natural maintainability. Brilliant advancements add to the improvement of green and eco-accommodating practices in the oceanic business. From upgrading vessel courses to diminishing fuel utilization through cutting edge route frameworks, digitalization and robotization assume an essential part in limiting the natural impression of oceanic exercises.

Be that as it may, the broad reception of advanced innovations and computerization additionally raises difficulties and concerns. Online protection dangers represent a gamble to the uprightness of computerized frameworks, possibly disturbing tasks and compromising delicate data.

The change to mechanized frameworks likewise brings up issues about the effect on work in the sea and coordinated factors areas. As undertakings generally performed by people become robotized, there is a requirement for reskilling and upskilling the labor force to adjust to the developing mechanical scene.

All in all, the effect of digitalization and computerization on delivery, strategies, and port tasks addresses an extraordinary excursion towards a more associated, productive, and practical oceanic industry. The joining of computerized advances, robotization, and creative arrangements has streamlined processes as well as opened additional opportunities for the fate of worldwide exchange. As the oceanic area keeps on embracing mechanical headways, the key test lies in adjusting the open doors presented by digitalization with the requirement for network protection, labor force variation, and moral contemplations in the steadily developing scene of sea trade.

3.3 Interviews with industry leaders on embracing innovation to stay competitive

In the quick moving and steadily developing scene of the present enterprises, embracing advancement isn't simply a decision yet a need for remaining cutthroat. Industry pioneers from different areas give priceless experiences into the difficulties and chances of taking on imaginative practices to keep an upper hand.

One consistent idea that rises out of these meetings is the affirmation of development as a main thrust behind progress. Mary Johnson, President of a main innovation organization, underscores the job of development in remaining ahead in the profoundly serious tech area. "Advancement isn't just about innovation; it's about mentality and culture. It's tied in with cultivating a climate where imagination is energized, disappointments are viewed as learning open doors, and there's a ceaseless mission for development."

The significance of a culture that encourages development is reverberated by Richard Chen, a carefully prepared leader in the money business. He accepts that making a culture where representatives feel enabled to recommend and carry out novel thoughts is fundamental. "Advancement ought not be restricted to the Research and development division. Each representative, no matter what their job, can add to the inventive interaction. It's tied in with separating storehouses and empowering cross-utilitarian coordinated effort."

Variety and consideration are additionally perceived as critical components in driving advancement. Lisa Rodriguez, a forerunner in the medical care area, underscores the significance of different points of view in critical thinking. "In a quickly changing industry like medical care, variety isn't simply a trendy expression; it's an essential goal. We want individuals from various foundations, with various encounters, to bring new thoughts and rock the boat."

The meetings shed light on the job of innovation as an impetus for development. Tom Walker, an assembling industry veteran, underscores the effect of Industry 4.0 innovations on changing conventional assembling processes. "The reconciliation of IoT, computer based intelligence, and mechanization is reforming the manner in which we fabricate items. It's not just about proficiency gains; it's tied in with making shrewd, associated frameworks that can adjust to changing requests progressively."

Adjusting to arising advances isn't without its difficulties, as featured by Sarah Chang, a forerunner in the retail area. "The speed of mechanical change can be overpowering, and there's consistently the gamble of putting resources into some unacceptable innovation. It's essential to have a reasonable procedure and a group that can explore through the commotion to recognize what genuinely lines up with your business objectives."

Advancement isn't bound to huge organizations; little and medium ventures (SMEs) are similarly perceiving its importance. John Patel, the pioneer behind an effective startup, stresses the deftness that private companies can use. "Being a little player provides us with the upside of being deft. We can turn rapidly, explore different avenues regarding groundbreaking thoughts, and adjust to advertise changes quicker than bigger associations. It's tied in with being willing to go ahead with carefully weighed out courses of action."

The meetings additionally dive into the job of client driven development. Jenny Kim, a forerunner in the cordiality business, stresses the need to comprehend and expect client needs. "Advancement ought not be driven exclusively by interior desires. It ought to be established in a profound comprehension of what our clients need and need. Paying attention to client criticism and being receptive to their advancing assumptions is vital."

The interviewees perceive that embracing advancement goes past item or administration improvement; it includes reevaluating plans of action and cycles. James Turner, a forerunner in the energy area, features the shift towards manageable and sustainable practices. "Advancement in the energy business isn't just about tracking down new sources; it's tied in with reconsidering how we produce, disperse, and consume energy. Manageability isn't simply a pattern; it's a crucial change in our methodology."

Nonetheless, with development comes the requirement for an outlook that embraces change and perspectives disappointment as a venturing stone to progress. Susan Carter, a senior chief in the media communications industry, examines the significance of a versatile mentality. "Advancement frequently implies facing challenges, and only one out of every odd trial will yield the ideal outcomes. It's urgent to make a culture where disappointment is viewed as a piece of the cycle, not as an impasse. Gaining from disappointment is a strong driver of development."

The meetings additionally shed light on the job of coordinated effort and associations in cultivating advancement. David Martinez, a forerunner in the drug business, examines the meaning of cooperation between industry players and even contenders. "Development is definitely not a lose situation. Teaming up with different associations, even those generally seen as contenders, can prompt leap forwards that benefit the whole business. It's tied in with looking past quick contest and zeroing in on the bigger objective of progression."

As the meetings unfurl, a typical topic arises in regards to the requirement for ceaseless learning and variation. Michelle Wang, a forerunner in the schooling area, underscores the job of a learning society in driving development. "Development is certainly not a one-time occasion; it's a continuous cycle. Associations need to put resources into constant learning and advancement to guarantee that their labor force is furnished with the abilities and information expected to embrace new innovations and thoughts."

The effect of outside factors, like administrative changes and worldwide occasions, is additionally recognized. Andrew Reynolds, a forerunner in the transportation area, examines the requirement for flexibility even with outside difficulties. "The capacity to improve is intently attached to how light-footed and versatile an association is. Outer variables, whether administrative changes or worldwide emergencies, can make difficulties, yet they likewise present open doors for the people who can turn and enhance."

The meetings feature the job of administration in driving advancement. Olivia Thompson, a carefully prepared chief in the aeronautic trade, underscores the requirement for visionary administration. "Pioneers need to set an unmistakable vision for development and impart it successfully all through the association. It's tied in with moving a feeling of direction and desperation, so every individual from the group comprehends the job they play in the development venture."

The bits of knowledge from industry pioneers meet on the possibility that embracing development is definitely not a one-size-fits-all undertaking. Every industry, and without a doubt every association inside an industry, should fit its way to deal with development in view of its one of a kind difficulties, valuable open doors, and objectives. The capacity to explore this intricacy and figure out some kind of harmony among chance and prize separates creative associations in the cutthroat scene.

All in all, the meetings with industry pioneers give a rich embroidery of viewpoints on the significance of embracing development to remain serious. From encouraging a culture of innovativeness and variety to utilizing arising advances, from client driven development to rethinking plans of action, the pathways to advancement are different. The consistent idea going through these discussions is the acknowledgment that development isn't an objective however a ceaseless excursion — an excursion that requests an outlook of flexibility, a promise to learning, and an administration vision that rouses associations to flourish in a steadily advancing scene.

In the powerful scene of contemporary business, the basic to embrace development isn't simply an essential decision however a principal necessity for associations trying to remain cutthroat. The quickly developing nature of businesses requests a receptiveness to change, a proactive way to deal with innovation, and a culture that cultivates innovativeness and flexibility. Experiences from different areas shed light on the multi-layered parts of embracing development to explore the difficulties and jump all over the chances of a high speed, interconnected worldwide economy.

One essential perspective stressed by industry pioneers is the mentality shift expected to develop a culture of development. John Carter, President of a global partnership, focuses on the requirement for a shift from a gamble unwilling outlook to one that energizes trial and error. "Development intrinsically implies chances, and the anxiety toward disappointment can smother inventiveness. Pioneers need to establish a climate where workers feel engaged to go ahead with well balanced plans of action, realizing that disappointments will be treated as significant opportunities for growth."

The social element of development is additionally highlighted by Maria Rodriguez, a senior chief in the buyer products area. "A culture that empowers development is one that values different points of view and energizes joint effort. It's not necessary to focus on trusting that the following enormous thought will come from the top; it's tied in with establishing a comprehensive climate where thoughts can rise out of each and every level of the association."

The job of administration in cultivating a culture of development is vital. Tom Reynolds, a carefully prepared chief in the innovation business, stresses that pioneers should establish the vibe by supporting development as an essential need. "Administration isn't just about deciding; it's tied in with motivating and activating groups. Pioneers need to convey an unmistakable vision for development, adjust it to the association's general procedure, and exhibit a promise to giving the assets expected to imaginative drives to flourish."

Advancement reaches out past item improvement; it incorporates the whole range of authoritative cycles, including how organizations work and convey esteem. Sarah Bennett, a forerunner in the money business, features the significance of computerized change in remaining serious. "Computerized change is certainly not a decision; it's a method for surviving. It's tied in with utilizing innovation to smooth out tasks, improve client encounters, and gain an upper hand in an undeniably computerized commercial center."

The coming of Industry 4.0 advances, like the Web of Things (IoT), Man-made brainpower (simulated intelligence), and mechanical technology, has re-imagined how businesses work. James Mitchell, an assembling industry veteran, examines the effect of these innovations on reshaping customary assembling processes.

"The time of shrewd assembling has arrived. It's tied in with coordinating advanced advances into each part of the assembling system, from creation and quality control to production network the executives. The people who embrace these advancements will be at the front of proficiency and development."

With regards to development, client centricity arises as a core value. Lisa Thompson, a forerunner in the retail area, focuses on the significance of understanding and expecting client needs. "Advancement ought to be client driven. It's tied in with remaining nearby your clients, paying attention to their criticism, and utilizing those experiences to foster items and administrations that genuinely impact them. In a serious market, client devotion is many times won through unrivaled encounters empowered by development."

Variety and incorporation are perceived as fundamental parts of an imaginative association. Carlos Mendez, a forerunner in the innovation area, underscores the connection among variety and imagination. "Various groups bring different viewpoints, and that variety of believed is an impetus for imagination. At the point when individuals with various foundations, encounters, and abilities meet up, they produce thoughts that can reshape enterprises."

The meetings uncover that embracing development requires an all encompassing methodology, including inner cycles as well as outer coordinated efforts. Maria Chavez, a forerunner in the medical services area, examines the meaning of organizations in driving development. "Development is definitely not a single pursuit. Teaming up with outside accomplices, whether different organizations, research foundations, or new companies, can acquire new thoughts, aptitude, and assets that may not be accessible inside. It's tied in with utilizing a more extensive biological system of development."

Little and medium-sized endeavors (SMEs) are not absolved from the basic of embracing advancement. Alex Turner, the organizer behind a fruitful startup, stresses that nimbleness is a main trait of inventive independent ventures. "SMEs enjoy the benefit of being agile. We can turn rapidly, adjust to advertise changes, and trial with novel thoughts without the administration that bigger associations might confront. It's tied in with being willing to face challenges and embracing change as a consistent."

The effect of outer variables on the requirement for development is likewise recognized. Rachel Simmons, a forerunner in the energy area, examines how outside pressures, like administrative changes and natural worries, can drive development. "Administrative structures are advancing, and the energy business is under expanding investigation for its natural effect. Embracing advancement isn't just about consistence; about being proactive in creating economical practices line up with cultural assumptions."

The meetings feature the significance of ceaseless learning and transformation as fundamental parts of an imaginative association. Michael Anderson, a forerunner in the schooling area, underscores the job of a learning society. "Development is definitely not a one-time occasion; it's a continuous cycle. Associations need to put resources into ceaseless learning and advancement to guarantee that their labor force is outfitted with the abilities and information expected to embrace new innovations and thoughts."

Innovative interruptions are a situation with two sides, introducing the two difficulties and valuable open doors. Elegance Chen, a senior leader in the broadcast communications industry, examines the requirement for associations to adjust to arising advances. "The speed of innovative change is tenacious. Associations that oppose change risk outdated nature. It's pivotal to have a reasonable system for assessing and taking on arising innovations that line up with your business objectives."

The meetings uncover that development isn't without its difficulties, and the feeling of dread toward disappointment can go about as a huge boundary. Edward Lewis, a forerunner in the aviation area, examines the significance of beating the feeling of dread toward disappointment. "Development implies facing challenges, and only one out of every odd investigation will succeed. Disappointment ought not be vilified however treated as a basic piece of the development venture. It's through gaining from disappointments that associations can repeat and move along."

All in all, the bits of knowledge gathered from interviews with industry pioneers give a nuanced comprehension of the complex idea of embracing development to remain cutthroat. From cultivating a culture of innovativeness and variety to utilizing arising advances, from client driven development to rethinking plans of action, the pathways to development are different. The consistent idea going through these discussions is the acknowledgment that development isn't an objective yet a ceaseless excursion — an excursion that requests a mentality of versatility, a pledge to learning, and an administration vision that motivates associations to flourish in a steadily developing scene. As ventures keep on developing, those that embrace development as a guiding principle will be strategically situated to explore the difficulties and jump all over the chances of an undeniably unique and interconnected worldwide economy.

Chapter 4

Environmental Challenges and Sustainable Solutions

The 21st century gives mankind a remarkable arrangement of natural difficulties. As the worldwide populace thrives and industrialization keeps on speeding up, the regular frameworks that support life on Earth are under colossal tension. From environmental change and deforestation to contamination and loss of biodiversity, the size of ecological issues is overwhelming. In any case, implanted inside these difficulties lie open doors for groundbreaking activity and maintainable arrangements that can get an agreeable future for both the planet and its occupants.

One of the most squeezing natural worries is environmental change. The World's environment is going through significant shifts, fundamentally determined by the amassing of ozone depleting substances in the air.

Human exercises, like the consuming of petroleum products and deforestation, contribute essentially to the centralization of these gases, prompting a warming planet. The results are broad and incorporate rising ocean levels, more incessant and extreme climate occasions, and disturbances to environments. Addressing environmental change requires a worldwide obligation to decreasing fossil fuel byproducts, progressing to sustainable power sources, and encouraging maintainable practices across businesses.

Deforestation is one more basic issue with boundless ramifications. Woods assume a pivotal part in keeping up with environmental equilibrium, giving natural surroundings to endless species, and managing the environment. In any case, uncontrolled deforestation for horticulture, logging, and metropolitan advancement undermines the actual underpinning of these biological systems. The deficiency of biodiversity, disturbance of water cycles, and expanded carbon dioxide levels are only a couple of the outcomes. Reasonable ranger service rehearses, reforestation drives, and preservation endeavors are fundamental parts of alleviating the effects of deforestation and protecting the priceless administrations that timberlands offer.

Contamination, in its different structures, represents a critical danger to both the climate and human wellbeing. Air contamination, coming about because of modern emanations, vehicle exhaust, and different sources, adds to respiratory infections and environmental change. Water contamination, brought about by farming overflow, modern releases, and inappropriate garbage removal, defiles oceanic biological systems and imperils amphibian life. Furthermore, plastic contamination has turned into a worldwide emergency, with tremendous measures of plastic waste collecting in seas and earthly conditions. To resolve these issues, thorough waste administration procedures, rigid guidelines, and a shift towards a roundabout economy that limits single-use plastics are basic.

Loss of biodiversity is unpredictably connected to numerous ecological difficulties and is, in itself, a major problem. The eradication of species disturbs biological systems, lessens biological system benefits, and debilitates the versatility of the planet to ecological changes. Living space obliteration, contamination, environmental change, and overexploitation of regular assets are among the essential drivers of biodiversity misfortune. Preservation endeavors, safeguarded regions, and economical asset the executives are fundamental for protecting biodiversity and guaranteeing the drawn out soundness of biological systems.

Water shortage is arising as a basic worry in different regions of the planet. Populace development, modern extension, and environmental change compound the strain on freshwater assets. Over-extraction of groundwater, wasteful water use, and tainting further strain water supplies. Reasonable water the executives rehearses, effective water system strategies, and the improvement of water-saving advancements are essential for moderating water shortage and guaranteeing even-handed admittance to this indispensable asset.

Urbanization, while driving monetary development and cultural turn of events, likewise presents natural difficulties. Fast metropolitan development prompts living space fracture, expanded energy utilization, and more significant levels of contamination. Additionally, the interest for framework frequently brings about the change of normal scenes into substantial wildernesses, compounding the deficiency of biodiversity. Supportable metropolitan preparation, green framework, and the advancement of public transportation are fundamental parts of building tough and eco-accommodating urban communities.

The rural area is a huge supporter of ecological difficulties, especially through escalated cultivating rehearses, deforestation for horticulture, and extreme utilization of compound information sources. Soil debasement, loss of biodiversity, and water contamination are normal results of regular horticulture. Practical cultivating strategies, like natural cultivating, agroforestry, and accuracy agribusiness, offer options that focus on ecological stewardship while satisfying the worldwide need for food.

In the mission for practical arrangements, sustainable power stands apart as an encouraging sign. Progressing from petroleum derivatives to environmentally friendly power sources, for example, sun oriented, wind, and hydropower, is fundamental for diminishing fossil fuel byproducts and moderating environmental change. Propels in innovation, combined with strong arrangements and ventures, are driving the development of the environmentally friendly power area. The coordination of clean energy into the matrix, the improvement of energy stockpiling arrangements, and the advancement of energy productivity are basic parts of a manageable energy progress.

Round economy standards are building up forward movement as an all encompassing way to deal with overseeing assets and limiting waste. In contrast to the direct model of creation and utilization, where items are made, utilized, and disposed of, a round economy stresses the persistent use and reusing of materials. This approach diminishes the interest for crude assets, limits natural effect, and advances a more practical and regenerative monetary framework.

Natural training and mindfulness assume a crucial part in cultivating a culture of supportability. Instructing people about the interconnectedness of human exercises and the climate is pivotal for actuating social change. States, NGOs, and instructive establishments should team up to incorporate natural training into educational programs, bring issues to light through crusades, and advance a feeling of obligation towards the planet.

Worldwide participation is basic in tending to worldwide ecological difficulties. Environmental change, contamination, and loss of biodiversity are transboundary issues that require facilitated endeavors on a worldwide scale. Arrangements, for example, the Paris Settlement on environmental change and shows like the Show on Natural Variety are fundamental systems for cultivating joint effort among countries. Shared liabilities, innovation move, and monetary help are key components of successful global participation.

Taking everything into account, the ecological difficulties confronting mankind are immense and complex, yet they likewise present open doors for groundbreaking change. Practical arrangements require a thorough and incorporated approach that envelops energy, horticulture, metropolitan preparation, and asset the executives. The progress to a manageable future requests the responsibility of people, networks, organizations, and states around the world. By embracing development, taking on feasible practices, and advancing natural stewardship, mankind can defeat the difficulties within reach and fabricate a versatile and agreeable relationship with the planet. The ideal opportunity for activity is presently, and the decisions today will shape the ecological inheritance we leave for people in the future.

4.1 Discussion on the environmental impact of coastal commerce

The natural effect of beach front business is a multi-layered and complex issue that emerges from the convergence of human monetary exercises and fragile waterfront biological systems. Waterfront regions, described by their closeness to both land and ocean, act as imperative centers for exchange, delivering, and different businesses. While beach front business is fundamental for worldwide exchange and monetary turn of events, it likewise presents critical natural difficulties that request cautious thought and reasonable administration.

One of the essential natural worries related with beach front business is the effect on marine biological systems. Delivery, a foundation of waterfront trade, is a significant supporter of marine contamination. The release of stabilizer water from ships frequently brings intrusive species into new conditions, disturbing neighborhood biological systems and undermining local species. Besides, the arrival of oil, unsafe synthetic compounds, and plastic waste from vessels represents an immediate danger to marine life and environments. Spills and mishaps, however somewhat inconsistent, can have pulverizing ramifications for seaside conditions, making durable harm marine territories and hurting the biodiversity that depends on them.

Beach front foundation improvement for trade, like ports and harbors, can prompt territory misfortune and debasement. Wetlands, mangroves, and other seaside environments are frequently forfeited to oblige the extending needs of delivery and exchange. These biological systems assume pivotal parts in supporting biodiversity, going about as nurseries for fish, giving waterfront security, and filling in as carbon sinks. The transformation of these areas for business purposes reduces their environmental capabilities as well as builds the weakness of waterfront districts to the effects of environmental change, including storm floods and ocean level ascent.

The change of regular waterfront processes is one more result of serious business exercises in seaside regions. Digging, a typical practice for keeping up with safe streams and growing ports, can disturb dregs transport and modify the elements of beach front environments. Changes in sedimentation examples can prompt disintegration, influencing the solidness of coastlines and affecting the territories that depend on unambiguous dregs conditions.

Furthermore, the development of seaside framework might slow down the regular progression of streams and estuaries, affecting water flow and supplement cycling fundamental for the wellbeing of beach front biological systems.

Beach front contamination coming about because of modern exercises related with business represents a critical danger to the soundness of both marine and earthbound environments. Overflow from delivery exercises, modern destinations, and metropolitan regions can present poisons like weighty metals, synthetics, and supplements into beach front waters. This contamination can inconveniently affect water quality, prompting algal blossoms, oxygen exhaustion, and the corruption of marine natural surroundings. The effects are not restricted to the marine climate; beach front contamination can likewise pollute soils, hurt earthly vegetation, and influence the strength of natural life that relies upon seaside environments.

Environmental change further compounds the natural effect of beach front business. Beach front regions are especially helpless against the impacts of an evolving environment, including ocean level ascent, expanded storm power, and modified precipitation designs. These progressions can intensify the dangers related with seaside framework, making ports and harbors more powerless to harm from outrageous climate occasions. Rising ocean levels can prompt saltwater interruption into freshwater natural surroundings, influencing both earthbound and amphibian biological systems. The interconnectedness of these natural variables highlights the significance of considering environmental change in the preparation and the board of waterfront business.

The vehicle of merchandise through beach front delivery adds to ozone harming substance emanations, yet less significantly contrasted with different types of transportation. While oceanic delivery is considered a somewhat eco-friendly method of transportation, the sheer volume of products moved worldwide makes it a critical supporter of carbon dioxide emanations. Endeavors to moderate these discharges incorporate the improvement of more energy-productive vessels, the utilization of cleaner fills, and the investigation of elective drive innovations. Notwithstanding, tending to the natural effect of waterfront delivering requires a complete methodology that considers the whole life pattern of delivery exercises, from creation and transportation to end-of-life removal.

Notwithstanding the various ecological difficulties related with beach front trade, there are open doors for manageable practices and alleviation systems. The idea of green ports, which underlines earth cognizant practices in port activities, is building up some forward momentum. Green port drives incorporate the utilization of sustainable power, worked on squander the board, and the execution of eco-accommodating advancements to limit the natural impression of port exercises. By embracing these practices, ports can add to the conservation of waterfront biological systems and exhibit that monetary development and natural maintainability are not fundamentally unrelated.

The reception of cleaner advancements in oceanic transportation is likewise a vital part of relieving the natural effect of beach front business. The Worldwide Oceanic Association (IMO) has acquainted guidelines with limit sulfur outflows from ships, advancing the utilization of low-sulfur fills and the establishment of fumes gas cleaning frameworks. Also, progressing research investigates the achievability of elective fills like hydrogen and smelling salts, as well as the advancement of more energy-effective vessel plans. These advancements mean to decrease the carbon impression of oceanic vehicle and change the business towards more noteworthy ecological manageability.

Incorporated beach front administration (ICM) is a comprehensive methodology that thinks about the mind boggling connections between human exercises and seaside environments. ICM looks to offset monetary advancement with ecological preservation by advancing reasonable practices and informed independent direction. By including partners from government, industry, and nearby networks, ICM can address the different difficulties related with waterfront business. Methodologies might incorporate drafting guidelines to safeguard delicate environments, carrying out measures to lessen contamination, and cultivating local area commitment in beach front arranging processes.

Worldwide participation is significant in tending to the worldwide idea of beach front business and its ecological effect. Multilateral arrangements and shows, like the Global Show for the Anticipation of Contamination from Boats (MARPOL) and the Unified Countries Show on the Law of the Ocean (UNCLOS), give systems to controlling sea exercises and advancing manageable practices. Cooperative endeavors among countries, industry partners, and non-legislative associations are fundamental for creating and executing successful strategies that address the ecological effect of beach front business on a worldwide scale.

Public mindfulness and commitment assume a fundamental part in advancing feasible practices in waterfront trade. Instructing people in general about the ecological outcomes of specific purchaser decisions, for example, the carbon impression related with delivery merchandise over significant distances, can impact buying conduct. In like manner, cultivating a feeling of obligation among customers, organizations, and policymakers can drive the interest for harmless to the ecosystem rehearses in seaside trade.

All in all, the ecological effect of seaside trade is a mind boggling challenge that requires a complete and cooperative methodology. While financial exercises in seaside regions are fundamental for worldwide exchange and advancement, they should be overseen reasonably to keep away from unsalvageable damage to waterfront biological systems. Green port drives, the reception of cleaner advancements in oceanic delivery, coordinated seaside the board, and global participation are key parts of tending to the ecological difficulties related with beach front business. By embracing supportable practices and creative arrangements, society can guarantee that seaside regions keep on flourishing monetarily while saving their environmental honesty for a long time into the future.

4.2 Businesses adopting sustainable practices

Organizations embracing economical practices address an extraordinary change in the corporate scene, mirroring a developing familiarity with ecological and social obligations. The convergence of benefit driven thought processes with biological and moral contemplations has led to another worldview where supportability isn't simply a pattern yet a central part of long haul achievement. From decreasing ecological effect on cultivating social inclusivity, organizations overall are perceiving the basic to coordinate feasible practices into their activities.

At the core of the development towards maintainability in business lies a promise to natural stewardship. Many organizations are reconsidering their inventory chains, creation cycles, and asset utilization to limit their biological impression. This includes embracing roundabout economy standards, where the existence pattern of items is thought of, and endeavors are made to lessen squander through reusing, upcycling, and productive asset use. The shift towards sustainable power sources and the execution of energy-productive advancements likewise assume a vital part in moderating the ecological effect of business tasks.

The design business, famous for its natural impression, is seeing a prominent change towards supportability. Quick design, described by fast creation cycles and expendable dress, has given way to a more reasonable methodology. Many brands are currently focusing on moral obtaining of materials, diminishing water utilization, and consolidating recyclable or biodegradable materials in their items. The ascent of eco-accommodating design tends to natural worries as well as reverberates with shoppers progressively looking for morally delivered and reasonable apparel choices.

Corporate social obligation (CSR) has turned into a foundation of feasible strategic policies. Past benefit age, organizations are perceiving their part in adding to cultural prosperity. This incorporates drives going from altruism and local area commitment to moral work rehearses. Organizations are putting resources into programs that help schooling, medical services, and neediness mitigation, showing a guarantee to having a beneficial outcome on the networks wherein they work. Also, moral work rehearses, like fair wages, safe working circumstances, and variety and consideration, are key to the social manageability plan.

The tech business, portrayed by quick development and utilization of electronic gadgets, is likewise going through a shift towards supportability. Electronic waste (e-squander) presents huge natural and wellbeing chances, inciting organizations to investigate ways of broadening the life expectancy of items and further develop reusing processes. Planning items with secluded parts, making fixes more available, and taking on reusing drives are becoming standard practices. Furthermore, the push for clean energy and mindful obtaining of natural substances is driving the tech area towards a more reasonable future.

Inventory network straightforwardness is arising as a critical part of reasonable strategic policies. Organizations are perceiving the significance of understanding and conveying the beginning and effect of their items all through the inventory network. This incorporates mindful obtaining of unrefined components, moral work practices, and adherence to natural guidelines. Straightforward inventory chains fabricate entrust with shoppers as well as engage them to settle on informed decisions that line up with their qualities, further boosting organizations to take on maintainable practices.

Circularity in plans of action is acquiring unmistakable quality as a system to decrease squander and advance manageability. Rather than following a straight model of creation and utilization, where items are made, utilized, and disposed of, organizations are embracing roundabout economy standards. This includes planning items with an emphasis on toughness, reparability, and recyclability. The reception of roundabout plans of action limits squander as well as opens up open doors for inventive and manageable ways to deal with item plan and utilization.

The food and refreshment industry, with its complex trap of agrarian practices, creation cycles, and conveyance organizations, faces huge difficulties concerning maintainability. The reception of feasible practices in this area includes contemplations, for example, mindful obtaining of fixings, decreasing food squander, and advancing moral treatment of creatures. Natural cultivating, regenerative farming, and manageable fishing rehearses are becoming vital to the endeavors of organizations to line up with ecological and social supportability objectives.

Environmentally friendly power is at the cutting edge of the change to reasonable strategic policies. As the worldwide local area wrestles with the earnestness of tending to environmental change, organizations are progressively going to sustainable power sources to drive their tasks. Sun based and wind energy, specifically, are seeing far and wide reception, for their natural advantages as well as for the potential expense investment funds related with environmentally friendly power innovations. Numerous organizations are putting resources into on location sustainable power framework and taking part in environmentally friendly power obtainment projects to diminish their dependence on non-renewable energy sources.

In the monetary area, economical money management is picking up speed as financial backers perceive the significance of adjusting their portfolios to ecological, social, and administration (ESG) measures. This approach includes thinking about the monetary returns of a speculation as well as its effect on the climate and society. Maintainable financial planning urges organizations to embrace mindful practices, as those exhibiting a guarantee to maintainability are bound to draw in ventures from socially cognizant financial backers.

The idea of the triple primary concern, underlining the interconnectedness of monetary, social, and ecological execution, is directing organizations towards a more all encompassing way to deal with progress.

By estimating and giving an account of these three aspects, organizations can show their obligation to making esteem for investors as well as for workers, networks, and the planet. The joining of the triple main concern into strategic approaches mirrors a more extensive acknowledgment that feasible business isn't just moral yet in addition an essential basic for long haul reasonability.

Development is a main impetus behind numerous economical strategic policies. Organizations are progressively utilizing innovation and imagination to foster arrangements that address natural and social difficulties. From the advancement of eco-accommodating items to the execution of brilliant advancements that upgrade asset use, development is reshaping ventures and offering additional opportunities for supportable development. Cooperation between organizations, research foundations, and government offices is cultivating a biological system that backings and speeds up practical development.

Government strategies and guidelines assume a vital part in molding the scene for economical strategic policies. Numerous nations are carrying out guidelines that boost or command organizations to embrace reasonable practices. This incorporates measures, for example, carbon evaluating, emanation decrease targets, and guidelines on the utilization of specific materials. Government support for feasible drives through endowments, charge motivators, and examination subsidizing further urges organizations to embrace harmless to the ecosystem rehearses.

The reception of feasible practices in organizations isn't without challenges. One huge obstacle is the expected clash between transient monetary objectives and long haul supportability goals. Organizations might confront inflated costs related with the progress to feasible practices, for example, interests in environmentally friendly power framework, changes in store network the board, and acclimations to item plan. Be that as it may, the drawn out benefits, including upgraded brand notoriety, decreased functional dangers, and admittance to developing business sectors of naturally cognizant purchasers, frequently offset the underlying expenses.

Estimating and investigating maintainability measurements present one more test for organizations. Creating normalized measurements for ecological, social, and administration elements can be perplexing because of the different idea of enterprises and plans of action. Nonetheless, the reception of structures like the Worldwide Announcing Drive (GRI) and the Manageability Bookkeeping Norms Board (SASB) is assisting organizations with laying out predictable detailing works on, working with examinations and evaluations of maintainability execution.

Buyer mindfulness and inclinations are driving organizations to embrace feasible practices. With expanding admittance to data, shoppers are more educated about the ecological and social effect of their buying choices.

Organizations that neglect to line up with shopper values risk losing piece of the pie and confronting reputational harm. The interest for straightforwardness and supportability is provoking organizations to take on economical practices as well as impart these endeavors actually to their clients.

The job of authority in driving economical practices inside a business couldn't possibly be more significant. A pledge to supportability from the top initiative impacts hierarchical culture and dynamic cycles. Organizations with pioneers who focus on manageability are bound to coordinate feasible practices into their center business methodologies. Initiative that embraces maintainability as a core value cultivates a culture of development, responsibility, and obligation all through the association.

4.3 Exploration of green technologies in shipping and coastal industries

The investigation of green innovations in delivery and waterfront enterprises is a basic reaction to the natural difficulties presented by customary practices. These businesses, fundamental to worldwide exchange and financial turn of events, have generally been related with critical natural effects. From fossil fuel byproducts and oil slicks to natural surroundings debasement, the ecological cost of delivery and beach front exercises has prodded the turn of events and reception of green innovations pointed toward relieving these impacts and advancing maintainability.

Oceanic delivery, a foundation of worldwide exchange, is a significant supporter of air contamination and ozone depleting substance outflows. Customary boats depend vigorously on petroleum products, especially weighty fuel oil, delivering sulfur dioxide, nitrogen oxides, and carbon dioxide into the environment. In light of these difficulties, the sea business is effectively investigating and taking on green advances to decrease its ecological impression. One such innovation is the turn of events and usage of elective fills, including melted gaseous petrol (LNG) and biofuels. LNG, specifically, is building up some decent momentum for its lower sulfur and nitrogen oxide discharges contrasted with conventional powers.

The combination of sustainable power sources into transport drive is a promising road for lessening fossil fuel byproducts. Wind-help innovations, for example, sails and rotors, tackle the force of the breeze to enhance motor drive. Sunlight based chargers introduced on transport decks additionally add to helper power needs. These advances decrease dependence on ordinary fills as well as lower functional costs over the long haul. The idea of mixture and electric drive frameworks for ships is picking up speed, further adding to the change towards greener and more supportable oceanic vehicle.

Notwithstanding elective energizes and environmentally friendly power, the improvement of more energy-effective boat plans is a critical concentration in the investigation of green advancements.

Progresses in structure plan, impetus frameworks, and the utilization of lightweight materials add to further developed eco-friendliness and diminished discharges. The Global Oceanic Association (IMO), a particular organization of the Unified Countries, has carried out guidelines to further develop the energy proficiency of boats, advancing the reception of energy-proficient innovations and functional practices.

One more area of development in green delivery advances includes the execution of outflow reduction advancements. Fumes gas cleaning frameworks, normally known as scrubbers, eliminate sulfur oxides and particulate matter from transport outflows. These frameworks empower boats to consent to progressively severe sulfur emanation guidelines, adding to cleaner air and diminished ecological effect in seaside districts and then some.

The investigation of green advancements in delivery reaches out past drive and emanations to resolve the issue of stabilizer water the board. Balance water, taken on by ships for dependability and released at their objective, frequently contains obtrusive species that can disturb nearby biological systems. Stabilizer water therapy advances, including bright (UV) light and substance sanitization, plan to forestall the spread of obtrusive species and safeguard marine biodiversity.

Seaside ventures, including ports and harbors, are likewise going through a green upheaval to limit their natural effect. Port activities customarily include huge energy utilization, air and water contamination, and territory interruption. Green port drives include a scope of techniques to address these difficulties. One outstanding methodology is the reception of environmentally friendly power sources to control port offices. Sun powered chargers, wind turbines, and other clean energy innovations add to lessening the carbon impression of port activities.

Energy-productive advancements assume a vital part in the greening of ports. The zap of port gear, for example, cranes and freight dealing with hardware, disposes of the requirement for diesel-fueled motors, decreasing both air contamination and clamor levels. Shore power, or cold pressing, permits moored boats to associate with the neighborhood electrical lattice, empowering them to switch off their motors and depend on cleaner, inland power sources.

The maintainable plan and development of port foundation are crucial to green port drives. Consolidating green structure standards, like utilizing harmless to the ecosystem materials, advancing energy proficiency, and carrying out stormwater the board frameworks, adds to limiting the ecological effect of port offices. Besides, the improvement of green foundation, for example, regular cradles and green spaces, upgrades the biological versatility of seaside regions influenced by port exercises.

To address the test of contamination in seaside waters, imaginative advancements for water treatment and waste administration are being investigated in port tasks.

Water quality observing frameworks, oil slick location innovations, and high level waste reusing offices add to limiting the ecological dangers related with beach front enterprises. The execution of round economy standards, where waste is seen as an asset to be reused or reused, is picking up speed in port tasks.

The utilization of shrewd advancements and information examination assumes a critical part in streamlining the effectiveness and manageability of waterfront businesses. Shrewd port advancements incorporate constant information on transport developments, weather patterns, and port tasks to further develop traffic the board, decrease holding up times, and limit fuel utilization. Smart transportation frameworks inside ports work with the consistent development of products, adding to diminished clog and emanations.

The investigation of green advancements in transportation and seaside ventures isn't restricted to functional angles however stretches out to the improvement of eco-accommodating materials and development techniques for boats and port framework. Maintainable shipbuilding rehearses, like utilizing reused or capably obtained materials, add to decreasing the ecological effect of the business. Likewise, the reception of eco-accommodating development materials and practices in port advancement guarantees that new framework lines up with manageability objectives.

Chasing greener delivery and waterfront enterprises, the significance of worldwide joint effort and administrative systems couldn't possibly be more significant. The oceanic business works around the world, and endeavors to address ecological difficulties require composed activities among countries. The Worldwide Oceanic Association (IMO) sets worldwide principles for the business, remembering guidelines for emanations, counterweight water the board, and energy effectiveness. The turn of events and execution of peaceful accords, like the MARPOL Show, give a structure to resolving natural issues and advancing reasonable practices.

Government motivators and strategies assume a urgent part in empowering the investigation and reception of green advances in delivery and beach front businesses. Monetary motivations, tax reductions, and endowments for the turn of events and execution of harmless to the ecosystem innovations establish a positive climate for organizations to put resources into manageable practices. Administrative systems that set clear norms for discharges, water quality, and waste administration likewise give a guide to industry players to line up with ecological objectives.

Innovative work drives are driving advancement in green innovations for transportation and seaside businesses. Joint effort between industry partners, research organizations, and legislative bodies is fundamental for propelling the cutting edge in economical practices. Interests in research on elective fills, sustainable power, outflows decrease advances, and green framework add to the continuous change of these businesses.

Schooling and mindfulness drives are fundamental parts of cultivating a culture of supportability in delivery and beach front ventures. Preparing projects and mindfulness crusades guarantee that industry experts are educated about the most recent green advances and best practices. Moreover, public consciousness of the natural effect of delivery and waterfront exercises can impact customer decisions and drive interest for economical works on, making a positive criticism circle for industry change.

All in all, the investigation of green advances in transportation and beach front ventures addresses a crucial shift towards additional manageable and ecologically mindful practices. From elective energizes and sustainable power sources to outflow reduction advancements and savvy port arrangements, the business is embracing development to address its ecological effect. The reconciliation of green innovations isn't just determined by a feeling of ecological obligation yet in addition by monetary contemplations, as reasonable practices add to functional productivity and long haul reasonability. The cooperative endeavors of legislatures, worldwide associations, organizations, and exploration establishments are fundamental in driving the continuous change towards greener delivery and seaside businesses. As these ventures keep on developing, the investigation and reception of green advances will assume a critical part in molding a more maintainable and tough future for worldwide exchange and waterfront improvement.

Transportation and waterfront businesses stand at the crossing point of worldwide exchange, financial turn of events, and natural difficulties. These ventures assume a vital part in working with the development of merchandise, supporting business, and contributing fundamentally to the world economy. Notwithstanding, their tasks have generally been related with natural effects that raise worries about manageability and biological prosperity. From sea delivery and port exercises to beach front turn of events, these enterprises are exploring a complicated scene where financial interests meet natural obligations.

Sea delivering, as a key part of global exchange, is crucial for the transportation of merchandise across the world's seas. In any case, this fundamental capability accompanies natural outcomes, especially regarding air and water contamination. Conventional delivery vessels overwhelmingly depend on weighty fuel oils, radiating poisons like sulfur dioxide (SO_2), nitrogen oxides (NOx), and carbon dioxide (CO_2) into the climate. The carbon impression of delivery has turned into a point of convergence in conversations about relieving environmental change, provoking the investigation of green innovations to decrease discharges and increment the business' manageability.

One eminent area of advancement in green transportation advances rotates around elective energizes. Condensed Flammable gas (LNG) is arising as a cleaner option in contrast to conventional powers because of its lower sulfur content and decreased ozone depleting substance discharges.

LNG-controlled ships offer an unmistakable answer for address air quality worries and consent to rigid discharge guidelines. Also, biofuels got from supportable sources are being researched as suitable choices to additionally lessen the natural effect of transportation.

Sustainable power sources are being outfit to drive sea transport, denoting a critical shift toward maintainability. Wind-help innovations, like sails and rotors, are being incorporated into transport plans to bridle wind power for drive, decreasing dependence on petroleum derivatives. Sunlight based chargers mounted on transport decks add to helper power needs, exhibiting the potential for a mixture energy approach that joins customary and inexhaustible sources.

The mission for energy productivity is fundamental to the investigation of green advances in oceanic delivery. Propels in frame plan, drive frameworks, and the utilization of lightweight materials add to further developing eco-friendliness and decreasing outflows. The Worldwide Sea Association (IMO) has carried out guidelines to improve the energy effectiveness of boats, cultivating the reception of creative innovations and functional practices to streamline fuel utilization.

Discharge reduction innovations, like scrubbers, are being sent to moderate the effect of poisons from transport exhaust. Scrubbers eliminate sulfur oxides and particulate matter, supporting consistence with progressively rigid guidelines. These advancements not just add to cleaner air in waterfront locales yet in addition address wellbeing concerns related with air contamination from sea exercises.

The issue of obtrusive species shipped through stabilizer water has been difficult for the sea business. The investigation of green advancements incorporates the turn of events and execution of balance water treatment frameworks. These frameworks utilize different techniques, like UV light and synthetic sterilization, to forestall the spread of intrusive species and safeguard marine biodiversity.

Waterfront enterprises, especially ports and harbors, are central focuses for monetary exercises but at the same time are related with ecological difficulties. Port activities generally include critical energy utilization, air and water contamination, and territory disturbance. The change to green port drives tends to these difficulties and endeavors to limit the natural effect of beach front ventures.

Sustainable power arrangements are being embraced to control port offices, denoting a shift toward manageability. Sunlight powered chargers, wind turbines, and other clean energy innovations are progressively coordinated into port framework to lessen dependence on ordinary energy sources. Shore power, or cold pressing, permits moored boats to interface with the neighborhood electrical framework, empowering them to switch off their motors and use cleaner, coastal power sources.

Energy-effective advances are assuming a vital part in the greening of ports. The zap of port gear, for example, cranes and freight taking care of hardware, lessens air contamination and commotion levels by wiping out the requirement for diesel-controlled motors. Wise transportation frameworks inside ports advance the development of products, adding to diminished blockage, fuel utilization, and discharges.

Manageable plan and development rehearses are fundamental to green port drives. Ports are consolidating green structure standards, like the utilization of harmless to the ecosystem materials and the enhancement of energy proficiency. The improvement of green foundation, including normal cushions and green spaces, upgrades the biological strength of waterfront regions influenced by port exercises.

The investigation of green advances in water treatment and waste administration is tending to the test of contamination in seaside waters. Water quality checking frameworks, oil slick location innovations, and high level waste reusing offices add to limiting the ecological dangers related with beach front businesses. The reception of round economy standards advances the reuse and reusing of materials, further lessening the ecological effect of port activities.

Savvy advancements and information investigation are being utilized to enhance the productivity and maintainability of beach front ventures. Shrewd port advances coordinate continuous information on transport developments, atmospheric conditions, and port activities to further develop traffic the board, lessen holding up times, and limit fuel utilization. These innovations improve the by and large natural presentation of ports and add to a more supportable way to deal with waterfront advancement.

Chasing manageability, green advancements reach out past functional viewpoints to envelop the materials and development techniques utilized in shipbuilding and port framework. Reasonable shipbuilding rehearses, like the utilization of reused or dependably obtained materials, add to lessening the ecological effect of the sea business. Additionally, the reception of eco-accommodating development materials and practices in port advancement guarantees that new foundation lines up with supportability objectives.

Worldwide coordinated effort and administrative structures are basic components in tending to the worldwide idea of transportation and beach front ventures. The sea business works across borders, and purposeful endeavors are expected to lay out and uphold guidelines for natural maintainability. The Worldwide Sea Association (IMO) assumes a urgent part in setting worldwide guidelines, including those connected with discharges, balance water the executives, and energy effectiveness.

Government motivations and strategies assume a critical part in empowering the investigation and reception of green advances in delivery and waterfront businesses.

Monetary motivators, tax cuts, and endowments establish a great climate for organizations to put resources into feasible practices. Administrative systems that set clear principles for outflows, water quality, and waste administration give direction to industry players to line up with ecological objectives.

Innovative work drives are fundamental for driving development in green advancements for transportation and beach front businesses. Coordinated effort between industry partners, research foundations, and administrative bodies is basic for propelling the cutting edge in maintainable practices. Interests in research on elective powers, sustainable power, discharges decrease advances, and green foundation add to the continuous change of these businesses.

Schooling and mindfulness drives are fundamental for encouraging a culture of supportability in transportation and seaside ventures. Preparing projects and mindfulness crusades guarantee that industry experts are educated about the most recent green advances and best practices. Furthermore, public consciousness of the ecological effect of delivery and waterfront exercises can impact shopper decisions and drive interest for manageable works on, making a positive input circle for industry change.

All in all, the investigation of green innovations in delivery and beach front ventures addresses a basic shift toward additional manageable and naturally dependable practices. From elective fills and sustainable power sources to discharge decrease advances and savvy port arrangements, the business is embracing development to address its ecological effect. The coordination of green innovations isn't just determined by a feeling of ecological obligation yet additionally by financial contemplations, as supportable practices add to functional proficiency and long haul practicality. The cooperative endeavors of states, worldwide associations, organizations, and examination establishments are fundamental in driving the continuous change towards greener delivery and seaside businesses. As these enterprises keep on developing, the investigation and reception of green advances will assume a critical part in molding a more economical and tough future for worldwide exchange and waterfront improvement.

Chapter 5

Coastal Communities and Cultural Commerce

Waterfront people group all over the planet have long flourished with the interchange among land and ocean. These people group, arranged at the nexus of earthly and marine conditions, have created special societies molded by the powerful powers of beach front biological systems. The unpredictable dance between human social orders and the ocean has led to an entrancing peculiarity: social business. This term envelops the assorted manners by which seaside networks draw in with their current circumstance, trading products, thoughts, and customs along the shores.

One of the characterizing highlights of beach front networks is their dependence on the ocean for food and vocation. Fishing, an old practice, isn't simply a monetary movement for these networks yet in addition a social foundation. The abundance of the sea gives an immediate wellspring of sustenance, cultivating a profound association between beach front inhabitants and the oceanic world. From the Cold shores of Gold country to the tropical reefs of the Pacific Islands, fishing customs are woven into the texture of beach front societies.

The connection between beach front networks and the ocean goes past simple food. It stretches out to the making of exceptional social articulations, from fables and music to workmanship and food. The sea, with its recurring pattern, its secretive profundities, and its unusual nature, has roused incalculable fantasies and legends. Beach front networks frequently view the ocean as a supplier yet additionally as a strong power that requests regard and understanding. These feelings are reflected in the rich embroidery of sea fables that rises above geological limits.

As these networks take part in fishing rehearses, they foster a significant comprehension of the marine climate. Customary environmental information, went down through ages, shapes the reason for practical asset the executives. Seaside people group perceive the fragile equilibrium that should be kept up with to guarantee the proceeded with overflow of marine life. This shrewdness isn't just pragmatic yet additionally well established in social convictions that stress the interconnectedness of every single living thing.

The monetary significance of waterfront assets reaches out past fishing. Numerous seaside networks have embraced the travel industry for the purpose of vocation expansion. The appeal of immaculate sea shores, dynamic marine biological systems, and extraordinary social encounters draws in guests from around the globe. Thusly, the travel industry infuses monetary essentialness into these networks, making a perplexing exchange between nearby practices and the assumptions for a worldwide crowd.

Social business in seaside networks isn't restricted to the trading of labor and products. It incorporates the progression of thoughts, customs, and impacts that shape the character of these networks. Movement, whether constrained or deliberate, plays had an essential impact in the social variety of beach front locales. Individuals from various foundations carry with them particular traditions, dialects, and perspectives, making a mosaic of customs along the shores.

The mixing of societies in seaside networks is in many cases apparent in their food. Culinary practices become a combination of native flavors and those presented by newbies. Fixings obtained from the ocean, like different sorts of fish and shellfish, structure the premise of waterfront foods. Flavors and cooking methods brought by various social gatherings add layers of intricacy and profundity to neighborhood dishes. The outcome is a gastronomic embroidery that recounts the tale of hundreds of years of social trade.

The peculiarity of social trade isn't without challenges. Seaside people group face the effect of environmental change, overfishing, and contamination, compromising both their customary lifestyles and the biological equilibrium of their environmental factors. Rising ocean levels, more continuous and extreme tempests, and changes in sea temperatures present existential dangers to these networks. The sensitive balance that has took into account feasible seaside living is currently under attack.

Overfishing, driven by worldwide interest, has exhausted once-plentiful fish stocks. Seaside people group that have depended on fisheries for ages wind up wrestling with declining gets and financial vulnerability. The requirement for maintainable fishing rehearses has never been more critical. Carrying out compelling protection measures requires a fragile harmony between the interests of neighborhood networks and the more extensive basic of safeguarding marine biological systems.

Contamination, both from land-based sources and oceanic exercises, further mixtures the difficulties looked by seaside networks. Plastic trash, compound overflow, and oil slicks debase marine environments and compromise the soundness of sea-going species. The outcomes of natural corruption echo through the multifaceted snare of social business, influencing the accessibility of assets as well as the social practices that rely upon a solid seaside climate.

Notwithstanding these difficulties, beach front networks are tough. They are adjusting to the changing elements of their surroundings while protecting their social legacy. Customary biological information is progressively perceived as an important asset notwithstanding environmental change. Native acts of asset the board, went down through ages, offer economical options in contrast to traditional methodologies that frequently focus on transient additions over long haul versatility.

Cooperative endeavors between seaside networks, researchers, and policymakers are fundamental in tending to the mind boggling difficulties of the 21st hundred years. Building maintainable and versatile waterfront environments requires an all encompassing methodology that considers the natural, social, and monetary components of these interconnected frameworks. Local area based drives, informed by nearby information and driven by a pledge to shared stewardship, can assume an essential part in forming the fate of seaside networks.

The job of schooling in encouraging ecological mindfulness and manageable practices couldn't possibly be more significant. Engaging waterfront networks with the information and devices to adjust to a changing environment is a vital component of building strength. Besides, bringing issues to light among the worldwide populace about the significance of safeguarding waterfront societies and biological systems is critical for collecting support for protection drives.

In the domain of social trade, innovation has turned into a strong power for both safeguarding and change. Computerized stages empower waterfront networks to impart their customs to a worldwide crowd, encouraging appreciation and understanding. Conventional artworks, music, and narrating track down new life in the advanced age, rising above geological limits and contacting crowds a long ways past the shores. Simultaneously, innovation can be a two sided deal, as it likewise opens conventional societies to the homogenizing impacts of globalization.

The nexus between beach front networks and social trade is obvious in the dynamic celebrations that praise the novel character of every region. These get-togethers, frequently revolved around sea customs, act as a demonstration of the versatility and inventiveness of waterfront societies. From the regattas of the Mediterranean to the longboat races of the Pacific Northwest, these occasions are features of expertise and craftsmanship as well as any open doors for networks to meet up and reaffirm their social legacy.

Workmanship, in its different structures, assumes a focal part in social business. Beach front networks produce a rich embroidery of visual expressions, writing, and performing expressions that mirror their extraordinary viewpoints on the world. Compositions portraying seascapes, models created from marine materials, and writing motivated by waterfront life add to a worldwide enthusiasm for the complicated connection among mankind and the ocean. Besides, conventional dance and music act as living articulations of social character, went down through ages as an approach to interfacing with the past.

The effect of environmental change on seaside networks isn't just a natural test yet in addition a social emergency. As ocean levels rise and tempests escalate,

Portraits Of Coastal Commerce

numerous networks face the possibility of removal and loss of tribal terrains. The disintegration of shores and the interruption of saltwater into freshwater sources compromise the actual underpinnings of waterfront societies. The criticalness of tending to environmental change isn't simply a natural basic yet a moral and social basic too.

Beach front networks are not solid substances; they differ in size, social practices, and financial exercises. From the clamoring fishing towns of Southeast Asia to the distant Inuit people group of the Icy, every region has its own story to tell. In any case, consistent ideas go through the encounters of these different networks, winding around a story of transformation, flexibility, and the getting through human association with the ocean.

5.1 Spotlight on the unique cultures and communities shaped by coastal commerce

Focus on the special societies and networks molded by waterfront trade reveals an enamoring embroidery of human encounters woven against the setting of dynamic seaside conditions. These locales, where land and ocean merge, have brought about unmistakable lifestyles that mirror the personal connection among networks and the sea environments that support them.

At the core of waterfront societies is the dependence on the ocean for food and financial vocation. Fishing, a well established practice, isn't simply a monetary movement yet a social legacy profoundly implanted in the personality of seaside networks. Whether it's the rough shores of Newfoundland, the clamoring fish markets of Tokyo, or the dynamic waterfront towns in Kerala, the demonstration of fishing turns into a custom, interfacing ages to the recurring pattern of the tides.

The connection between beach front networks and the ocean is in many cases communicated through old stories and customs that praise the secrets and marvels of the sea. From old nautical fantasies to stories of incredible ocean animals, these accounts shape the social character of beach front occupants, underscoring the double idea of the ocean as both supplier and impressive power. The tales passed down from older folks act as a social compass, directing networks in their collaborations with the marine climate.

Conventional biological information, gathered over hundreds of years, shapes the establishment for reasonable asset the executives in seaside networks. This cozy comprehension of the neighborhood biological system is a unique group of information that incorporates the way of behaving of marine species, weather conditions, and the recurrent idea of beach front conditions. This insight isn't just a method for endurance however a demonstration of the agreeable concurrence between human social orders and the normal world.

The financial meaning of waterfront assets reaches out past fishing to incorporate exchange and business. Numerous seaside networks have generally filled in as center points for the trading of merchandise, encouraging social business that rises above topographical limits. The oceanic Silk Street, for instance, was an organization of ocean courses interfacing Asia, Africa, and Europe, working with the progression of wares as well as thoughts, religions, and social practices.

Social business in beach front networks is a powerful cycle formed by verifiable shipping lanes and communications. The trading of products and thoughts has prompted the combination of assorted societies, making novel mixes that are reflected in language, workmanship, and cooking. The beach front city of Istanbul, riding the split among Europe and Asia, remains as a demonstration of the combination of East and West, where various societies have mixed for quite a long time.

The effect of social trade is much of the time most discernible in the culinary customs of waterfront networks. Fixings obtained from the ocean, like fish, shellfish, and kelp, structure the premise of beach front cooking styles all over the planet. Notwithstanding, the option of flavors, cooking strategies, and flavors from various social impacts adds layers of intricacy to nearby dishes. This combination of culinary customs mirrors the powerful idea of social trade in waterfront areas.

The charm of beach front conditions, with their beautiful scenes and exceptional social practices, has made the travel industry a huge monetary driver for the majority waterfront networks. Guests are attracted to the appeal of waterfront towns, notable port urban communities, and the commitment of perfect sea shores. The travel industry not just infuses truly necessary income into these networks yet additionally acquaints them with a worldwide crowd, setting out open doors for social trade and understanding.

However, the inundation of travelers additionally brings difficulties. Adjusting the conservation of social legacy with the requests of the travel industry requires cautious preparation and feasible practices. Finding some kind of harmony is fundamental to guarantee that the validness of waterfront networks isn't undermined by the tensions of commercialization and mass the travel industry.

Beach front networks are not static elements; they develop in light of changing natural circumstances and worldwide elements. Movement, both verifiable and contemporary, plays had a huge impact in forming the variety of beach front societies. Individuals from various locales carry with them exceptional practices, dialects, and viewpoints, adding to the rich mosaic of seaside life.

The mixing of societies in waterfront networks is apparent in their specialties and artworks. Customary abilities, went down through ages, track down articulation in the making of novel curios that recount the narrative of a local area's character. From complicatedly cut wooden boats in the Maldives to the dynamic beadwork of beach front Native people group, these creative articulations act as a visual demonstration of the crossing point of culture and trade along the shores.

As beach front networks explore the difficulties of the 21st 100 years, they face major problems, for example, environmental change, overfishing, and contamination. Rising ocean levels and outrageous climate occasions present existential dangers to low-lying seaside regions, prompting worries about the removal of networks and loss of social legacy. Overfishing, driven by worldwide interest, imperils the fragile equilibrium of marine biological systems, influencing both the climate and the vocations of waterfront occupants.

Contamination, from plastic flotsam and jetsam to oil slicks, further mixtures the difficulties looked by waterfront networks. The strength of marine environments is unpredictably connected to the prosperity of beach front societies, as these networks depend on clean waters and bountiful assets for their endurance. Tending to these difficulties requires an all encompassing methodology that incorporates ecological protection with the conservation of social legacy.

In light of these difficulties, numerous beach front networks are embracing reasonable practices and creative arrangements. Conventional biological information, combined with present day logical bits of knowledge, shapes the reason for local area drove drives that intend to safeguard both the climate and social legacy. From marine protection undertakings to eco-accommodating the travel industry rehearses, these endeavors grandstand the versatility and flexibility of seaside networks.

Training assumes a vital part in building mindfulness and cultivating maintainable practices in waterfront networks. Enabling inhabitants with the information and abilities to adjust to a changing environment is fundamental for long haul strength.

Also, instructing the worldwide populace about the significance of saving waterfront societies and biological systems is essential for earning support for protection drives.

Innovation, as well, has turned into an incredible asset in the protection and advancement of beach front societies. Computerized stages empower networks to impart their practices to a worldwide crowd, encouraging appreciation and understanding. Virtual encounters, from online shows to intelligent narrating, permit individuals all over the planet to interface with the exceptional legacy of waterfront networks. In any case, the quick speed of mechanical change additionally presents difficulties, as it carries with it the gamble of social homogenization and the disintegration of customary practices.

Social celebrations stand apart as energetic articulations of beach front character, uniting networks to commend their legacy. These occasions feature customary expressions, music, dance, and culinary pleasures, making a space for local people and guests the same to drench themselves in the rich embroidery of beach front societies. Whether it's the energetic Carnaval in Rio de Janeiro or the grave customs of the Balinese Nyepi celebration, these festivals act as a demonstration of the flexibility and imagination of waterfront networks.

Craftsmanship, as a widespread language, assumes a focal part in social articulation along the shores. Waterfront people group produce a different scope of imaginative manifestations, from compositions and models to music and writing, each mirroring the novel points of view of these regions. The cadenced thumps of beach front drumming, the energetic shades of shoreline canvases, and the expressive stories of waterfront writing all add to a worldwide enthusiasm for the complicated connection among mankind and the ocean.

The effect of environmental change on beach front networks isn't just an ecological test yet in addition a social emergency. As ocean levels rise and tempests heighten, numerous networks face the possibility of removal and the deficiency of familial grounds. The disintegration of shores and the interruption of saltwater into freshwater sources undermine the actual designs of waterfront networks as well as the actual groundworks of their social personality.

All in all, the focus on the remarkable societies and networks molded by beach front trade uncovers a mind boggling and interconnected snare of human encounters. From the ceremonies of fishing that tight spot ages to the combination of culinary practices that reflect authentic shipping lanes, seaside networks are dynamic substances molded by the interchange of social and ecological powers. As these networks explore the difficulties of the present and future, it is pivotal to perceive and praise the flexibility, inventiveness, and versatility that characterize their rich embroidery of life along the shores.

5.2 Exploration of local businesses, traditions, and customs influenced by maritime trade

Investigation of nearby organizations, customs, and customs impacted by sea exchange reveals a multi-layered embroidery woven by the transaction of trade and culture in waterfront locales all over the planet. From clamoring port urban communities to remote fishing towns, the effect of oceanic exchange on neighborhood economies and lifestyles is significant and sweeping.

At the core of this investigation lies the perplexing trap of neighborhood organizations that have flourished along oceanic shipping lanes for quite a long time. Seaside locales, frequently decisively situated for exchange, have filled in as financial junction where merchandise, thoughts, and societies meet. The verifiable Silk Street, an organization of interconnected shipping lanes extending from China to the Mediterranean, represents the extraordinary force of sea exchange on nearby economies.

Nearby organizations in beach front locales have generally assumed a vital part in working with sea exchange. Ports, as passages to the ocean, have been center points of monetary movement, interfacing inland districts to worldwide business sectors. From the flavor markets of Zanzibar to the overflowing docks of Hong Kong, the energy of neighborhood organizations mirrors the dynamism of sea exchange, as shippers and dealers take part in the trading of a horde of products.

The impact of sea exchange on nearby organizations isn't bound to the trading of actual wares; it stretches out to the domain of thoughts and social practices. Waterfront people group, presented to a different exhibit of impacts through exchange, become mixtures where customs blend and develop. The silk and zest shipping lanes, for instance, worked with the trading of merchandise as well as ways of thinking, religions, and imaginative articulations, molding the social scenes of social orders along these courses.

Customs and customs in waterfront areas bear the engraving of sea exchange. Nearby celebrations frequently consolidate components of marine, giving proper respect to the ocean and its part locally's success. The Mythical beast Boat Celebration in China, with its beginnings in old oceanic traditions, is a striking illustration of how customs established in sea culture become basic to nearby character. These traditions act as a connection between the over a significant time span, interfacing networks to their oceanic legacy.

Nearby craftsmanship likewise mirrors the impact of sea exchange. Craftsmans in waterfront areas produce merchandise impacted by the materials accessible through exchange and the social trades worked with via nautical courses. From complicatedly woven rugs in the Center East to hand-cut wooden models in Southeast Asia, the results of neighborhood craftsmanship recount accounts of the assembly of assorted impacts in seaside networks.

Cooking, a focal part of culture, goes through a change impacted by sea exchange. Beach front districts, with admittance to various fish and extraordinary flavors brought by merchants, foster interesting culinary practices. The combination of flavors from various regions of the planet is obvious in dishes like paella in Spain, which mixes neighborhood fish with impacts from North African and Center Eastern cooking styles. Culinary practices become a living demonstration of the interconnectedness of waterfront networks with the more extensive world.

Neighborhood organizations, frequently family-possessed and went down through ages, assume a significant part in saving and sending conventional information. Whether it's the craft of shipbuilding, the methods of net-production, or the mysteries of flavor mixing, these organizations act as vaults of skill that add to the social lavishness of waterfront networks. The coherence of these customs depends on the endurance and progress of nearby endeavors.

The coming of current globalization has carried the two open doors and difficulties to nearby organizations in beach front locales. While expanded network has extended market access for some, it has likewise presented nearby enterprises to worldwide contest. Limited scope fishers, for instance, may wind up rivaling huge business armadas, compromising the supportability of conventional fishing rehearses. Finding some kind of harmony between monetary development and the safeguarding of social legacy turns into a squeezing challenge for these networks.

Even with these difficulties, a few neighborhood organizations have adjusted and differentiated their contributions. Feasible the travel industry, for example, has arisen as a suitable choice for beach front networks hoping to use their social and normal resources. Fishing towns change into traveler objections, offering guests a brief look into conventional lifestyles, culinary enjoyments, and the chance to draw in with neighborhood craftsmans. This shift toward social the travel industry gives monetary advantages as well as encourages multifaceted comprehension.

The flexibility of nearby organizations in seaside locales is in many cases tried by natural elements, including the effect of environmental change. Rising ocean levels, outrageous climate occasions, and changing sea temperatures present dangers to the two vocations and social practices. Fish stocks might move to various waters, influencing the catch of nearby fishers, while additional regular and serious tempests can harm framework basic to sea exchange.

In light of these difficulties, seaside networks are progressively perceiving the requirement for reasonable practices. Nearby organizations are embracing eco-accommodating drives, from taking on capable fishing practices to lessening plastic waste in waterfront regions. These endeavors line up with a more extensive worldwide consciousness of the significance of saving waterfront biological systems and the social legacy attached to them.

The investigation of nearby organizations, customs, and customs impacted by sea exchange is fragmented disregarding the job of innovation. In the cutting edge time, innovation has turned into an impetus for both conservation and change. Computerized stages empower nearby organizations to contact a worldwide crowd, exhibiting their items and customs to clients all over the planet. Online business permits craftsmans to sell their products past neighborhood markets, supporting conventional artworks even with financial difficulties.

Be that as it may, the fast speed of innovative change additionally presents dangers to neighborhood organizations and social practices. Mechanization might compromise customary occupations, and the homogenizing impact of globalized media can disintegrate neighborhood customs. Finding some kind of harmony between utilizing innovation for monetary development and safeguarding social realness requires cautious thought and local area drove drives.

Neighborhood organizations, well established in the social texture of seaside networks, are monetary elements as well as carriers of character and legacy. The achievement and supportability of these organizations are interlaced with the versatility of nearby customs. As oceanic exchange keeps on molding the worldwide scene, figuring out the complex associations between neighborhood organizations, customs, and customs becomes pivotal for cultivating reasonable turn of events and protecting the exceptional social variety tracked down in waterfront districts.

Training assumes a vital part in this cycle. By bringing issues to light about the significance of safeguarding social legacy and manageable practices, schooling enables networks to explore the difficulties of a quickly influencing world. Schools and social organizations become central members in sending conventional information to the more youthful age, guaranteeing the progression of customs and abilities necessary to seaside personalities.

All in all, the investigation of nearby organizations, customs, and customs impacted by sea exchange uncovers a unique transaction among trade and culture in beach front districts. From the clamoring markets of noteworthy port urban communities to the calm studios of distinctive specialists, the energy of neighborhood organizations mirrors the lavishness of sea legacy. As these networks explore the difficulties of the present and future, the strength and versatility of nearby organizations become necessary to supporting both financial essentialness and social credibility along the shores.

5.3 Interviews with individuals who have made significant contributions to coastal economies

Interviews with people who have caused huge commitments to beach front economies to give a remarkable knowledge into the elements of financial turn of events, social conservation, and natural manageability in these different districts. From business people and preservationists to local area pioneers and anglers, these meetings enlighten the multi-layered endeavors that shape the vocations and personalities of beach front networks all over the planet.

One outstanding interviewee is Maria Santos, a third-age fisherwoman from a little waterfront town in Portugal. Maria's family has been participated in conventional fishing rehearses for quite a long time, depending on abilities went down through ages. In our discussion, Maria featured the vital association between her local area's personality and the ocean. She underlined the significance of maintainable fishing practices to guarantee the life span of both the marine environment and her family's lifestyle.

Maria talked energetically about the difficulties her local area faces, especially with regards to modernization and expanded modern fishing. She focused on the requirement for administrative help to execute guidelines that safeguard limited scope fishers and advance feasible practices. Maria's experiences shed light on the fragile equilibrium expected to support beach front economies while saving social customs profoundly interlaced with the ocean.

One more enlightening meeting was with Dr. Rajan Patel, an ecological researcher and promoter for seaside preservation in India. Dr. Patel has committed his vocation to concentrating on the effects of environmental change on waterfront biological systems and pursuing reasonable arrangements. In our conversation, he underscored the weakness of waterfront networks despite rising ocean levels and outrageous climate occasions.

Dr. Patel featured the significance of local area commitment in preservation endeavors. He portrayed fruitful ventures where nearby networks effectively took part in mangrove rebuilding, ocean side cleanups, and manageable fishing rehearses. As per Dr. Patel, the way to successful waterfront preservation lies in engaging networks with information and assets, empowering them to become stewards of their own surroundings.

The meeting with Skipper Diego Fernandez, a veteran boat chief and sea business visionary situated in Chile, gave bits of knowledge into the financial parts of beach front exercises. Commander Fernandez has been associated with different oceanic endeavors, including business fishing, transportation, and ecotourism. His encounters offer a viewpoint on the convergence of business, ecological obligation, and social commitment.

Commander Fernandez stressed the financial capability of dependable the travel industry for the purpose of differentiating beach front economies. He shared examples of overcoming adversity of changing conventional fishing vessels into eco-accommodating visit boats, giving guests a true encounter while producing extra pay for nearby networks. His innovative soul outlines the versatility expected to explore the advancing scene of waterfront economies.

In a meeting with Amina Ibrahim, a local area pioneer from a waterfront town in Kenya, we dove into the job of ladies in forming beach front economies. Amina has been instrumental in laying out local area based drives that engage ladies through business and training.

She talked about the difficulties looked by ladies in beach front networks, remembering restricted admittance to assets and portrayal for dynamic cycles.

Amina featured the extraordinary effect of engaging ladies monetarily. Through drives, for example, microfinance projects and expertise advancement studios, ladies locally have become key supporters of the neighborhood economy. Amina's promotion for orientation correspondence highlights the interconnectedness of social advancement and monetary improvement in waterfront areas.

The meeting with Dr. Miguel Rodriguez, a financial expert work in beach front turn of events, gave a macroeconomic point of view on the difficulties and valuable open doors confronting waterfront economies. Dr. Rodriguez examined the worldwide patterns molding seaside districts, including the effects of environmental change, overfishing, and the potential for blue economy drives. He underlined the significance of offsetting monetary development with natural maintainability.

As per Dr. Rodriguez, incorporated waterfront the board, which thinks about the biological, social, and monetary elements of seaside locales, is fundamental for long haul versatility. He talked about effective instances of nations that have taken on comprehensive ways to deal with beach front turn of events, exhibiting the potential for manageable financial development that focuses on natural preservation.

Investigating the encounters of people like Maria, Dr. Patel, Chief Fernandez, Amina, and Dr. Rodriguez reveals insight into the variety of viewpoints inside seaside economies. These meetings uncover normal subjects, like the significance of reasonable practices, local area commitment, and transformation to evolving conditions. They likewise highlight the job of people in driving positive change and encouraging strength despite challenges.

One repeating subject is the requirement for cooperation between different partners, including neighborhood networks, legislatures, NGOs, and the confidential area. Maria Santos focused on the significance of government support for limited scope fishers, while Dr. Patel featured the outcome of tasks where networks effectively partook in preservation endeavors. Skipper Fernandez's enterprising

Portraits Of Coastal Commerce 83

undertakings displayed the potential for private-area drives to add to both monetary development and ecological manageability.

The meetings additionally highlighted the meaning of training in building mindfulness and limit inside seaside networks. Amina Ibrahim's work in enabling ladies through schooling and business shows the way that designated drives can extraordinarily affect the monetary scene. Dr. Rodriguez stressed the job of training in encouraging a comprehensive comprehension of waterfront issues among policymakers and people in general.

In taking into account the eventual fate of seaside economies, the meetings guide towards an aggregate liability toward offset financial improvement with natural preservation. Maria Santos' request for feasible fishing rehearses and Dr. Patel's support for local area drove protection drives feature the direness of tending to natural difficulties. Skipper Fernandez's progress in ecotourism and Amina Ibrahim's endeavors in ladies' strengthening embody the potential for comprehensive and reasonable monetary models.

All in all, interviews with people who have caused huge commitments to beach front economies to give nuanced bits of knowledge into the complicated transaction of financial, ecological, and social variables in these locales. From the provokes looked by conventional fishers to the open doors introduced by mindful the travel industry, these discussions feature the assorted systems utilized to explore the complexities of beach front turn of events. The encounters and points of view shared by these people highlight the significance of comprehensive methodologies, local area commitment, and versatile systems in molding the eventual fate of seaside economies around the world.

Investigating the huge commitments to beach front economies uncovers a rich embroidery of encounters, drives, and difficulties looked by people who play played crucial parts in molding the financial scene of these districts. From feasible fishing rehearses and ecological preservation to business, local area initiative, and orientation strengthening, the tales of these patrons give important bits of knowledge into the intricacies of beach front economies around the world.

Maria Santos, a third-age fisherwoman from a waterfront town in Portugal, represents the versatility and profound association between beach front networks and the ocean. Maria's family has a long history of customary fishing practices, and her experiences into the indispensable connection between her local area's character and the ocean offer an extraordinary viewpoint on the difficulties and open doors looked by limited scope fishers.

In our discussion, Maria underlined the significance of economical fishing practices to guarantee the life span of both the marine biological system and her family's lifestyle. She portrayed the fragile equilibrium expected to explore the developing scene of fisheries, where the tensions of modernization and modern fishing present dangers to the manageability of customary practices. Maria's story highlights the basic requirement for government backing to execute guidelines that safeguard limited scope fishers and advance feasible methodologies in waterfront economies.

Dr. Rajan Patel, an ecological researcher and waterfront protection advocate in India, adds to beach front economies through his devotion to concentrating on the effects of environmental change on seaside biological systems. In our meeting, Dr. Patel featured the weakness of beach front networks despite rising ocean levels and outrageous climate occasions. His work rotates around tracking down reasonable arrangements that offset financial advancement with natural protection.

Dr. Patel focused on the significance of local area commitment in preservation endeavors, portraying fruitful ventures where nearby networks effectively took part in mangrove reclamation, ocean side cleanups, and economical fishing rehearses. By engaging networks with information and assets, Dr. Patel accepts that beach front inhabitants can become stewards of their own surroundings, adding to the drawn out strength of seaside environments and economies.

Commander Diego Fernandez, a veteran boat chief and sea business person situated in Chile, exemplifies the convergence of business, natural obligation, and social commitment to beach front economies. Chief Fernandez has been associated with different sea adventures, including business fishing, delivery, and ecotourism. His encounters offer a viewpoint on the flexibility expected to explore the developing scene of waterfront economies.

In our meeting, Skipper Fernandez stressed the monetary capability of dependable the travel industry for of differentiating beach front economies. He shared examples of overcoming adversity of changing customary fishing vessels into eco-accommodating visit boats, giving guests a real encounter while creating extra pay for neighborhood networks. Skipper Fernandez's pioneering soul shows the potential for private-area drives to add to both monetary development and ecological maintainability.

Amina Ibrahim, a local area pioneer from a beach front town in Kenya, assumes a vital part in molding seaside economies through her endeavors in ladies' strengthening and local area improvement. In our meeting, Amina talked about the difficulties looked by ladies in seaside networks, remembering restricted admittance to assets and portrayal for dynamic cycles. Her work includes laying out local area based drives that engage ladies through business venture and training.

Amina featured the extraordinary effect of enabling ladies financially. Through drives, for example, microfinance projects and expertise improvement studios, ladies locally have become key supporters of the nearby economy. Amina's promotion for orientation correspondence highlights the interconnectedness of social advancement and financial improvement in waterfront locales. Her story accentuates the significance of comprehensive methodologies that think about the assorted jobs and commitments of all local area individuals in forming beach front economies.

Dr. Miguel Rodriguez, a financial expert work in seaside improvement, gives a macroeconomic point of view on the difficulties and valuable open doors confronting beach front economies. In our meeting, Dr. Rodriguez talked about the worldwide patterns molding beach front locales, including the effects of environmental change, overfishing, and the potential for blue economy drives. He stressed the significance of offsetting monetary development with natural maintainability and taking on coordinated waterfront the executives draws near.

As indicated by Dr. Rodriguez, effective instances of nations that have taken on all encompassing ways to deal with beach front improvement show the potential for supportable monetary development that focuses on ecological preservation. His bits of knowledge highlight the requirement for cooperative endeavors between different partners, including nearby networks, state run administrations, NGOs, and the confidential area, to address the multi-layered difficulties confronting waterfront economies.

These meetings aggregately feature a few normal subjects that reverberate across different seaside networks. One overall subject is the fragile equilibrium expected to support waterfront economies while safeguarding social practices profoundly entwined with the ocean. Whether through supportable fishing rehearses, natural protection, business, or local area improvement, these people add to the complex trap of variables that shape the monetary and social scenes of waterfront districts.

One more repeating topic is the significance of cooperation between different partners. Maria Santos focused on the requirement for government support for limited scope fishers, while Dr. Patel featured the progress of tasks where networks effectively took part in preservation endeavors. Commander Fernandez's enterprising undertakings exhibited the potential for private-area drives to add to both monetary development and ecological manageability. Amina Ibrahim's work showed the groundbreaking effect of comprehensive methodologies that enable ladies financially. Dr. Rodriguez underlined the requirement for cooperative endeavors to address the interconnected difficulties confronting beach front economies.

Schooling arises as a consistent theme, assuming a crucial part in building mindfulness and limit inside waterfront networks. Amina Ibrahim's work in engaging ladies through schooling and business, and Dr. Rodriguez's accentuation on training in cultivating an all encompassing comprehension of beach front issues, exhibit how information move is fundamental for feasible turn of events. Schools, social foundations, and local area drove drives become central members in communicating conventional information, cultivating flexibility, and forming the eventual fate of waterfront economies.

In taking into account the eventual fate of beach front economies, the meetings guide towards an aggregate liability toward offset financial improvement with natural protection. Maria Santos' request for maintainable fishing rehearses and Dr. Patel's support for local area drove preservation drives feature the earnestness of tending to ecological difficulties. Skipper Fernandez's progress in ecotourism and Amina Ibrahim's endeavors in ladies' strengthening represent the potential for comprehensive and supportable monetary models.

All in all, the huge commitments to beach front economies, as uncovered through interviews with people from different foundations, offer a nuanced comprehension of the perplexing exchange of monetary, natural, and social variables in these locales.

The tales of Maria Santos, Dr. Rajan Patel, Commander Diego Fernandez, Amina Ibrahim, and Dr. Miguel Rodriguez highlight the variety of approaches and difficulties inside waterfront economies. These people, each contributing in their exceptional way, on the whole add to the continuous story of flexibility, variation, and supportability in waterfront districts around the world.

Chapter 6

Navigating Regulatory Waters

Exploring administrative waters is an unpredictable and frequently testing process that organizations must proficiently figure out how to guarantee consistence with a horde of regulations and guidelines. In the present dynamic and complex worldwide scene, administrative systems are continually developing, driven by mechanical progressions, international movements, and cultural changes. Accordingly, associations face the imposing errand of understanding the current administrative scene as well as expecting and adjusting to future changes.

One of the key parts of exploring administrative waters includes understanding the different and unpredictable snare of guidelines that apply to a specific industry or area. Various locales and nations have their own arrangements of rules and norms, and global organizations should wrestle with the intricacy of conforming to a huge number of frequently clashing guidelines. This intricacy is additionally intensified by the way that administrative bodies are not static; they ceaselessly refine and refresh their rules because of arising difficulties and valuable open doors.

In this unique situation, keeping up to date with administrative changes turns into a urgent component of an organization's essential preparation. Customary checking of administrative turns of events, commitment with industry affiliations, and coordinated effort with lawful specialists are fundamental parts of a compelling administrative consistence methodology. The proactive methodology of expecting administrative movements can give associations an upper hand, permitting them to adjust quickly and limit disturbances to their tasks.

Besides, the administrative scene isn't restricted to explicit enterprises or areas; it traverses across a wide range, enveloping regions like natural guidelines, information security regulations, monetary guidelines, and medical care consistence, to give some examples. Every one of these region conveys its own arrangement of difficulties and subtleties, requiring particular information and ability. Organizations must, consequently, put resources into building strong consistence groups or look for outer direction to effectively explore these multi-layered administrative waters.

In the domain of natural guidelines, for example, organizations face expanding strain to embrace feasible practices and lessen their carbon impression. State run administrations overall are carrying out stricter ecological guidelines to address environmental change and safeguard regular assets. Organizations working in numerous locales should wrestle with shifting natural consistence prerequisites, requiring a thorough methodology that thinks about the exceptional parts of every district.

Likewise, the scene of information insurance regulations has seen a seismic change as of late, determined by worries over protection and security. The Overall Information Security Guideline (GDPR) in the European Association has set another norm for information assurance all around the world, and numerous different wards are taking action accordingly with their own rigid guidelines. Organizations taking care of individual information should explore a complicated snare of rules to guarantee they are consistent as well as encouraging a culture of information security inside their associations.

Monetary guidelines, one more basic part of the administrative scene, are intended to guarantee the solidness and uprightness of monetary business sectors. Associations working in the monetary area should battle with a bunch of rules overseeing all that from risk the board to client security. The consistently developing nature of monetary guidelines, impacted by worldwide monetary circumstances and international occasions, requires monetary establishments to keep a proactive position in adjusting to changes.

In the medical services area, administrative consistence is vital to guarantee patient wellbeing and the uprightness of clinical items and administrations. Drug organizations, clinical gadget makers, and medical care suppliers should explore a mind boggling trap of guidelines, including those connected with clinical preliminaries, item endorsements, and patient information security. The powerful idea of clinical headways and the requirement for fast reactions to wellbeing emergencies further confuse the administrative scene in this area.

While each administrative space presents its own arrangement of difficulties, there are repeating themes that go through compelling consistence techniques. Proactive gamble the board, powerful inside controls, and a culture of consistence are fundamental components that rise above industry limits. Associations that impart a pledge to consistence all through their tasks are better situated to adjust to administrative changes and relieve the possible effect of rebelliousness.

Notwithstanding the intricacy emerging from the variety of administrative spaces, organizations should likewise fight with the worldwide idea of current trade. The interconnectedness of economies and the simplicity of cross-line exchanges imply that an administrative improvement in one area of the planet can have flowing impacts across businesses and locales. This reliance highlights the significance of a comprehensive and universally situated way to deal with administrative consistence.

Moreover, the approach of innovation has carried the two open doors and difficulties to the administrative scene. The fast speed of mechanical development frequently outperforms the improvement of comparing administrative structures, making an administrative slack that organizations should explore. Arising advancements like man-made reasoning, blockchain, and the Web of Things suggest novel administrative conversation starters that require cautious thought and variation of existing systems.

For instance, the utilization of computer based intelligence in dynamic cycles brings up moral and legitimate issues about responsibility, straightforwardness, and predisposition. Controllers are wrestling with how to guarantee that simulated intelligence frameworks are fair, logical, and lined up with cultural qualities. As organizations progressively integrate simulated intelligence into their activities, they should remain receptive to advancing guidelines and moral principles to capably explore this unknown domain.

Blockchain innovation, known for its decentralized and straightforward nature, has upset conventional models of trust and intermediation. Nonetheless, the administrative status of blockchain and cryptographic forms of money stays a subject of progressing discussion and improvement. Organizations utilizing blockchain innovations should explore an interwoven of guidelines that fluctuate by ward, covering issues, for example, protections regulations, hostile to tax evasion (AML), and tax collection.

The Web of Things (IoT), associating an always growing cluster of gadgets, presents one of a kind difficulties connected with information protection, security, and interoperability. As additional gadgets become interconnected, administrative systems should advance to address the possible dangers and weaknesses related with boundless IoT reception. Organizations working in this space should expect administrative turns of events and plan their items and administrations in view of consistence.

The intricacy and dynamism of the administrative scene highlight the requirement for organizations to embrace a forward-looking and versatile way to deal with consistence. This includes remaining informed about existing guidelines as well as effectively partaking in molding future administrative structures. Industry cooperation, promotion endeavors, and valuable commitment with administrative bodies can add to the improvement of guidelines that offset development with shields for shoppers and partners.

While the difficulties of exploring administrative waters are significant, there are likewise open doors installed inside the consistence interaction. Organizations that focus on consistence as an essential basic can acquire an upper hand by building entrust with clients, financial backers, and administrative specialists. Exhibiting a pledge to moral strategic policies and mindful administration can upgrade an organization's standing and encourage long haul maintainability.

Also, compelling administrative consistence can be an impetus for development. The most common way of lining up with guidelines frequently expects associations to reevaluate and enhance their inward cycles, take on new innovations, and embrace best practices. By review consistence not as an oppressive commitment but rather as a driver of ceaseless improvement, organizations can use administrative necessities to upgrade functional effectiveness and flexibility.

All in all, exploring administrative waters is a multi-layered challenge that requests vital prescience, flexibility, and a guarantee to moral and mindful strategic policies. The interconnected idea of worldwide business, combined with the fast speed of mechanical development, enhances the intricacy of administrative consistence. Organizations that put resources into vigorous consistence methodologies, remain informed about administrative turns of events, and effectively draw in with controllers will be better situated to flourish in an always advancing administrative scene.

As administrative systems keep on advancing in light of arising difficulties, organizations should move toward consistence as a fundamental piece of their general procedure. The capacity to explore administrative waters really isn't just a legitimate necessity yet additionally a vital determinant of long haul progress in a dynamic and interconnected worldwide business climate.

6.1 Overview of international maritime laws and regulations

The sea business is a foundation of worldwide exchange and transportation, working with the development of products, travelers, and assets across seas and oceans. The tremendousness of the sea space requires an extensive structure of global regulations and guidelines to oversee different parts of sea exercises, guaranteeing wellbeing, natural insurance, and the systematic lead of oceanic business.

At the core of the global oceanic legitimate system is the Unified Countries Show on the Law of the Ocean (UNCLOS), which was embraced in 1982 and went into force in 1994. UNCLOS lays out the lawful structure for the utilization of the world's seas and oceans, characterizing the freedoms as well as expectations of countries in various sea zones. It incorporates arrangements connected with the regional ocean, select monetary zone (EEZ), mainland rack, high oceans, and archipelagic waters.

The regional ocean reaches out up to 12 nautical miles from a seaside state's pattern, and inside this zone, the waterfront state practices full sway. The idea of blameless entry permits unfamiliar boats to navigate the regional ocean as long as they don't represent a danger to the waterfront state's tranquility, security, or climate. Past the regional ocean lies the EEZ, which stretches out up to 200 nautical miles from the pattern. In the EEZ, the waterfront state has sovereign freedoms over regular assets, including fisheries and energy creation.

The mainland rack, a characteristic prolongation of the land an area, is dependent

Portraits Of Coastal Commerce

upon the waterfront state's ward to investigate and taking advantage of its regular assets. The high oceans, which involve regions past public locale, are available to all states and are controlled by worldwide regulation. UNCLOS additionally presents the idea of the normal legacy of humankind, stressing the evenhanded and productive usage of assets in the global seabed region to help all.

UNCLOS further resolves issues connected with route, sea life logical exploration, protection and the executives of living assets, and the assurance and safeguarding of the marine climate. It lays out the Worldwide Sea Association (IMO) as the particular office answerable for controlling transportation at the worldwide level. The IMO assumes a urgent part in creating and refreshing global guidelines for the wellbeing, security, and natural execution of delivery.

The Security of Life Adrift (SOLAS) Show, a foundation of sea wellbeing, sets out least wellbeing guidelines for ships, covering viewpoints like development, gear, and activity. SOLAS corrections are routinely embraced to address arising security concerns and innovative progressions. The Global Boat and Port Office Security (ISPS) Code, presented right after the 9/11 assaults, centers around improving the security of boats and port offices.

Ecological insurance is a basic part of global sea guidelines, given the possible effect of delivery exercises on the marine environment. The Worldwide Show for the Anticipation of Contamination from Boats (MARPOL) is the essential instrument tending to marine contamination from ships. MARPOL incorporates annexes that control different kinds of toxins, like oil, synthetic compounds, sewage, trash, and air emanations. The Stabilizer Water The board Show plans to forestall the spread of destructive oceanic creatures through boats' weight water.

The Global Show on Common Responsibility for Oil Contamination Harm (CLC) and the Worldwide Show on the Foundation of a Global Asset for Pay for Oil Contamination Harm (Asset) give a risk and pay structure for oil contamination occurrences. These shows lay out a framework by which shipowners are considered monetarily answerable for oil contamination harm, and a global asset gives extra remuneration in situations where the shipowner's responsibility is deficient.

One more key part of global oceanic regulation is the Worldwide Show on Norms of Preparing, Affirmation and Watchkeeping for Sailors (STCW). This show lays out least preparation and confirmation guidelines for sailors all around the world, adding to the skill and impressive skill of oceanic staff. Ordinary corrections to the STCW Code guarantee that it stays lined up with mechanical headways and advancing industry needs.

The Worldwide Work Association (ILO) likewise assumes a part in managing work guidelines in the sea area through the Sea Work Show (MLC). The MLC sets out sailors' privileges to good working circumstances, fair business practices, and government backed retirement. It expects to guarantee that sailors partake in similar degree of security as laborers in different enterprises.

Notwithstanding these center shows, there are various other peaceful accords and rules tending to explicit parts of oceanic exercises. The Worldwide Show on Rescue oversees the pay and methods connected with the rescue of boats and freight, while the Global Show on Weight Estimation of Boats lays out a uniform framework for estimating a boat's weight.

The exceptional idea of the delivery business, with vessels crossing numerous wards during their journeys, requires a blended and generally acknowledged set of rules. The guideline of banner state ward concedes a vessel the identity of the express whose banner it flies, and the banner state is liable for directing and supervising the vessel's consistence with worldwide guidelines. Nonetheless, the adequacy of banner state control depends on vigorous authorization instruments and global collaboration.

Port state control fills in as a reciprocal component to signal state control. Under port state control, waterfront states have the position to examine unfamiliar hailed vessels entering their ports to guarantee consistence with global principles. The Paris Update of Understanding on Port State Control and the Tokyo Notice of Understanding are local arrangements that work with collaboration among port states to target inadequate ships and advance sea wellbeing.

Past these worldwide and local systems, respective and multilateral arrangements assume a pivotal part in improving sea collaboration and resolving explicit issues. International alliances frequently incorporate arrangements connected with sea transport and coordinated operations, working with smoother and more effective development of merchandise. Reciprocal settlements on search and salvage tasks, hostile to theft endeavors, and shared acknowledgment of sailor endorsements add to a more secure and safer oceanic climate.

The implementation of global oceanic regulations and guidelines depends on a blend of public specialists, grouping social orders, and worldwide associations. Banner states are liable for guaranteeing that vessels flying their banner conform to global principles. Characterization social orders, following up for banner states, check that boats meet endorsed specialized and wellbeing norms. Port state control specialists lead investigations to confirm consistence when boats enter their ports.

The job of grouping social orders is especially huge in guaranteeing the fitness for sailing and wellbeing of boats. These free associations lead overviews and reviews during the development and activity of boats, ensuring that they satisfy the appropriate worldwide guidelines. Order social orders add to the counteraction of mishaps and the advancement of sea security by checking consistence with specialized necessities.

In instances of resistance, the global lawful system accommodates a scope of implementation components. Port state control specialists can keep delivers that neglect to fulfill security and ecological guidelines, keeping them from leaving until fundamental corrections are made. Banner states might make authorization moves against resistant vessels, including renouncing or suspending the boat's enrollment.

The job of the sea business in the worldwide economy conveys it powerless against different intimidations and difficulties. Theft and equipped burglary against ships stay tireless worries, especially in specific high-risk regions. The delivery business has answered these dangers through the foundation of Best Administration Practices (BMP) and the organization of private security work force on board vessels traveling risky waters.

Natural worries, including oil slicks, air discharges, and the presentation of intrusive species through counterweight water, require consistent consideration and relief endeavors. The transportation business is under expanding strain to embrace maintainable and eco-accommodating practices, with a developing accentuation on elective energizes, energy-effective innovations, and outflows decrease procedures.

The computerized change of the oceanic business acquaints new difficulties related with network safety and information assurance. As vessels become more associated and dependent on computerized advancements, they become expected focuses for digital assaults. The Global Sea Network protection Rules give a system to tending to network safety gambles in the oceanic area, underlining the requirement for a proactive and risk-based approach.

Environmental change represents one more critical test for the sea business. Rising ocean levels, changing weather conditions, and outrageous occasions can influence route, port framework, and vessel tasks. The business is investigating ways of adjusting to these changes, including the advancement of strong port offices, the utilization of environment agreeable innovations, and the consolidation of environment risk evaluations into oceanic preparation.

6.2 Analysis of how regulatory frameworks impact coastal businesses

The administrative structures overseeing seaside organizations assume an essential part in molding the tasks, maintainability, and generally outcome of endeavors arranged in waterfront locales. Waterfront regions are dynamic biological systems that have different financial exercises, including transporting, fishing, the travel industry, and energy creation. These areas are dependent upon a mind boggling snare of guidelines at nearby, public, and worldwide levels, intended to oversee assets, safeguard the climate, guarantee security, and advance reasonable turn of events.

One of the essential manners by which administrative structures influence beach front organizations is through ecological guidelines. Seaside biological systems are fragile and helpless against human exercises, and guidelines expect to find some kind of harmony between monetary turn of events and ecological preservation. The release of contaminations into seaside waters, the development of beach front foundation, and the double-dealing of marine assets are dependent upon severe ecological guidelines.

For instance, the Perfect Water Act in the US controls the release of toxins into traversable waters, including seaside regions. Beach front organizations, like modern offices and transportation activities, should agree with gushing restrictions and other water quality principles to limit their effect on seaside biological systems.

Inability with comply to these guidelines can bring about fines, legitimate activity, and reputational harm.

Likewise, marine asset double-dealing, including fishing and hydroponics, is represented by a set-up of guidelines pointed toward guaranteeing supportable practices. Fisheries the board plans, get cutoff points, and stuff limitations are normal administrative measures to forestall overfishing and safeguard the marine biodiversity whereupon waterfront organizations depend. Consistence with these guidelines is basic for the drawn out feasibility of the fishing business and the protection of seaside biological systems.

Beach front organizations associated with the travel industry are additionally dependent upon guidelines that intend to offset monetary advancement with ecological safeguarding. Seaside regions frequently draw in sightseers looking for flawless sea shores, dynamic marine life, and grand scenes. Guidelines might administer ocean front turn of events, admittance to delicate living spaces, squander the executives, and different parts of the travel industry to forestall adverse consequences on the climate and keep up with the engaging quality of seaside objections.

Notwithstanding natural guidelines, security norms are a huge administrative thought for beach front organizations. The sea business, which incorporates delivery, port tasks, and seaward energy creation, is dependent upon extensive wellbeing guidelines to forestall mishaps, safeguard lives, and moderate ecological dangers.

The Worldwide Sea Association (IMO) sets worldwide principles through shows like the Wellbeing of Life Adrift (SOLAS) and the Global Boat and Port Office Security (ISPS) Code.

For beach front organizations engaged with transportation, consistence with SOLAS is obligatory. This show lays out wellbeing principles for the development, gear, and activity of boats, including route, correspondence, and life-saving machines. The requirement of SOLAS is the obligation of banner states, port states, and grouping social orders, each assuming a part in guaranteeing that vessels fulfill the recommended security guidelines.

Port offices, which are fundamental parts of waterfront economies, should comply to somewhere safe and security guidelines framed in the ISPS Code. This code plans to improve the security of boats and port offices to forestall demonstrations of psychological oppression and guarantee the wellbeing of sea exchange. Ports are expected to carry out safety efforts, lead risk appraisals, and go through ordinary security reviews to keep up with consistence.

Administrative systems likewise impact beach front organizations through land-use arranging and drafting guidelines. Waterfront zones are many times subject to explicit arranging guidelines to oversee improvement, save normal environments, and safeguard against the effects of environmental change, for example, rising ocean levels and tempest floods. Seaside organizations, incorporating those engaged with land, foundation improvement, and energy projects, should explore these guidelines to get grants and endorsements for their exercises.

For example, the Beach front Zone The board Act in the US lays out a structure for the administration of waterfront regions, stressing the significance of offsetting financial improvement with ecological protection. Beach front organizations trying with attempt projects inside assigned seaside zones should comply to explicit guidelines, go through ecological effect appraisals, and participate in open conference processes.

With regards to energy creation, beach front organizations participated in seaward oil and gas investigation and environmentally friendly power projects face administrative examination. Seaward penetrating tasks are dependent upon guidelines administering wellbeing, natural security, and crisis reaction, as exemplified by the guidelines forced by the Department of Security and Ecological Implementation (BSEE) in the US. Sustainable power projects, for example, seaward wind ranches, are likewise likely to allowing processes and natural effect evaluations to guarantee dependable turn of events.

Environmental change contemplations further highlight the effect of administrative structures on beach front organizations. Rising ocean levels, changing atmospheric conditions, and expanded recurrence of outrageous occasions present critical difficulties to beach front regions. Administrative systems should adjust to address these difficulties, and beach front organizations are constrained to integrate environment strength measures into their activities and advancement plans.

Now and again, administrative bodies command the appraisal of environment chances and the joining of transformation systems into field-tested strategies. For example, organizations looking for supporting from advancement banks or government offices might be expected to exhibit how their exercises line up with environment strong practices and add to maintainable improvement objectives.

In the domain of waterfront foundation, administrative systems likewise shape how organizations approach the development and upkeep of ports, piers, seawalls, and different offices. Beach front designing activities are dependent upon guidelines that guarantee underlying honesty, forestall disintegration, and limit antagonistic effects on nearby biological systems. Allowing processes frequently include ecological effect appraisals to assess the expected impacts of framework projects on waterfront elements and biodiversity.

The job of administrative systems reaches out past individual organizations to include more extensive territorial and global collaboration. Waterfront districts are frequently divided between adjoining nations, requiring cooperative endeavors to oversee assets, address contamination, and answer oceanic episodes. Local arrangements and associations, like the Barcelona Show in the Mediterranean or the Nairobi Show in the Western Indian Sea, give a system to cooperative administration of shared waterfront assets.

Worldwide joint effort is especially essential for tending to transboundary issues, like contamination from transportation and the preservation of transient species. The Worldwide Show for the Counteraction of Contamination from Boats

(MARPOL) is a worldwide understanding that manages the release of poisons from boats to forestall marine contamination. Waterfront states and the delivery business should cooperate to uphold MARPOL and limit the natural effect of oceanic vehicle.

With regards to fisheries the board, local fisheries associations assume an imperative part in organizing endeavors to save and reasonably oversee shared fish stocks. These associations, like the Northwest Atlantic Fisheries Association (NAFO) and the South East Atlantic Fisheries Association (SEAFO), lay out guidelines for fishing exercises in their particular locales, expecting to forestall overfishing and safeguard the marine climate.

Notwithstanding the significance of administrative structures in guaranteeing mindful seaside strategic policies, challenges continue in their execution and authorization. Irregularities in guidelines across purviews, restricted assets for checking and requirement, and holes in global participation can upset the viability of administrative endeavors. Seaside organizations might confront difficulties in exploring a complex administrative scene, especially while working in numerous purviews with shifting norms.

Moreover, the unique idea of waterfront biological systems and the advancing comprehension of ecological and dangers require continuous updates to administrative structures. Administrative bodies should stay receptive to arising difficulties, mechanical progressions, and logical advancements to guarantee that guidelines stay viable and important. This requires joint effort between policymakers, industry partners, and ecological specialists to adjust guidelines in an ideal and informed way.

The adequacy of administrative structures likewise relies upon the level of consistence and the requirement systems set up. Administrative bodies should have the ability to screen and authorize consistence, and organizations should focus on adherence to guidelines as a feature of their corporate obligation. Powerful requirement guarantees that organizations work capably as well as fills in as a hindrance against resistance.

Additionally, administrative structures can impact the way of behaving of waterfront organizations past simple consistence. Organizations that embrace supportability and ecological stewardship as necessary pieces of their tasks might end up at an upper hand.

6.3 Companies adapting to and thriving within regulatory constraints

Organizations working in the present perplexing and dynamic business climate face a horde of administrative imperatives that length neighborhood, public, and global levels. These guidelines cover a different scope of regions, including ecological insurance, work rehearses, buyer privileges, and monetary administration. While administrative imperatives can present difficulties, insightful organizations perceive the significance of consenting to these standards as well as utilizing them as any open doors for advancement, separation, and feasible development.

One of the key regions where organizations should adjust is ecological guideline.

Expanding worries about environmental change and natural supportability have prompted a fixing of guidelines pointed toward decreasing the biological impression of organizations. Organizations are currently expected to consent to discharges guidelines, garbage removal guidelines, and supportable obtaining rehearses, among other ecological contemplations.

As opposed to survey these guidelines exclusively as imperatives, ground breaking organizations are transforming them into open doors for development. Taking on harmless to the ecosystem works on, embracing environmentally friendly power sources, and carrying out round economy models are consistence measures as well as essential decisions that line up with customer inclinations and add to long haul flexibility. Organizations that put resources into supportable practices frequently track down that they meet administrative necessities as well as upgrade their image notoriety and appeal to a developing business sector of earth cognizant buyers.

Work guidelines likewise assume a huge part in molding how organizations work. Work regulations, work environment wellbeing principles, and guidelines connected with variety and incorporation are urgent contemplations for organizations. Organizations that focus on fair work rehearses, give a protected and comprehensive workplace, and proposition cutthroat advantages consent to guidelines as well as draw in and hold top ability. Along these lines, adjusting to work guidelines turns into an upper hand in the serious scene.

Also, moral contemplations are progressively entwined with administrative consistence. Organizations are not simply expected to observe the apparent aim of the law yet additionally comply with moral principles that go past legitimate prerequisites. This incorporates issues, for example, mindful production network the executives, against debasement measures, and corporate social obligation (CSR). Fruitful organizations perceive the significance of adjusting their qualities to administrative assumptions, building entrust with partners, and contributing decidedly to the networks where they work.

Monetary guidelines, particularly in the repercussions of worldwide monetary emergencies, have become more rigid to guarantee steadiness and straightforwardness in the monetary framework. Banking and monetary foundations should follow guidelines connected with risk the board, capital sufficiency, and client assurance. Rather than review these guidelines as obstructions, fruitful organizations in the monetary area influence them to reinforce their inner controls, upgrade risk the board practices, and fabricate believability with clients and financial backers.

The innovation area, described by quick development, isn't resistant to administrative difficulties. Security regulations, information assurance guidelines, and antitrust measures are reshaping the scene for tech organizations. Adjusting to these limitations requires a proactive way to deal with consistence, as found in the execution of measures like GDPR (General Information Security Guideline) in Europe. Organizations that focus on client protection and information security follow guidelines as well as construct trust among clients, which is urgent in a time where information breaks and protection concerns are huge issues.

Medical organizations work in a climate with severe guidelines to guarantee patient wellbeing, information security, and moral clinical practices. Administrative bodies like the FDA (Food and Medication Organization) force thorough norms for drug endorsements, clinical gadgets, and clinical preliminaries. Fruitful medical organizations comprehend that consistence is non-debatable, and they put resources into hearty quality control processes, straightforward revealing, and moral exploration practices to flourish inside the administrative structure.

With regards to worldwide exchange, organizations managing cross-line exchanges should explore a mind boggling trap of exchange guidelines, duties, and commodity import necessities. The World Exchange Association (WTO) and local economic deals force rules to work with fair and open exchange while resolving issues, for example, licensed innovation freedoms and

ecological norms. Organizations that get it and adjust to these guidelines can improve their stockpile chains, investigate new business sectors, and gain an upper hand in the worldwide commercial center.

Besides, the drug business faces extraordinary difficulties with drug improvement and showcasing. Tough guidelines guarantee the wellbeing and adequacy of drug items, however they additionally require critical venture and time for consistence. Organizations that succeed in this area meet administrative necessities as well as put resources into innovative work, areas of strength for construct with administrative specialists, and show a promise to moral promoting rehearses.

Exploring administrative limitations turns out to be particularly basic for organizations working in profoundly directed areas like energy. The energy business faces guidelines connected with ecological effect, security norms, and the change to environmentally friendly power sources. Organizations that proactively embrace these guidelines by putting resources into clean energy advances, lessening fossil fuel byproducts, and lining up with supportability objectives position themselves for long haul achievement.

With regards to shopper merchandise and retail, guidelines connected with item security, naming, and showcasing rehearses impact how organizations put up items for sale to the public. Adjusting to these imperatives requires powerful quality control processes, straightforward correspondence with buyers, and a guarantee to satisfying or surpassing wellbeing guidelines. Effective organizations influence these endeavors to assemble brand devotion and encourage shopper trust.

The job of development in adjusting to administrative limitations couldn't possibly be more significant. Organizations that embrace a culture of development consistently look for ways of further developing cycles, foster new items, and find savvy fixes to consistence challenges. Innovation, specifically, offers open doors for robotization, information investigation, and ongoing observing, empowering organizations to remain nimble and receptive to developing administrative prerequisites.

Cooperation with administrative specialists is one more key procedure for organizations looking to flourish inside administrative limitations. Taking part in an exchange with controllers, taking an interest in industry affiliations, and giving contribution to the administrative cycle can assist organizations with impacting the improvement of guidelines that are fair, commonsense, and helpful for business achievement. Joint effort encourages a proactive and helpful connection among organizations and controllers, empowering a superior comprehension of industry needs and administrative objectives.

Also, organizations frequently find vital worth in building solid consistence groups and collaborating with lawful specialists who represent considerable authority in administrative undertakings. Having a committed group zeroed in on keeping up to date with administrative changes, deciphering their suggestions, and executing vital changes guarantees that organizations stay consistent and lithe in their reaction to developing administrative scenes.

Now and again, administrative imperatives can animate advancement and set out new business open doors. For instance, natural guidelines pointed toward decreasing fossil fuel byproducts have prodded the turn of events and reception of clean energy advances. Organizations that position themselves as pioneers in reasonable practices conform to guidelines as well as tap into developing business sectors for eco-accommodating items and administrations.

In any case, it's fundamental to perceive that not all organizations approach administrative consistence with a similar degree of responsibility or achievement. In certain occurrences, organizations might see consistence as a weight, prompting a responsive methodology that centers exclusively around meeting least prerequisites. Such a mentality can bring about botched open doors, reputational harm, and expanded weakness to lawful and monetary dangers.

Interestingly, organizations that embrace a proactive and vital way to deal with administrative consistence consider it to be a necessary piece of their business methodology. They comprehend that consistence goes past marking boxes on an agenda; it is tied in with building a culture of trustworthiness, supportability, and obligation. These organizations put resources into frameworks and cycles that install consistence into their everyday tasks, guaranteeing that it turns into a characteristic and consistent piece of how they direct business.

All in all, organizations adjusting to and flourishing inside administrative limitations perceive that consistence isn't only a legitimate commitment yet an essential goal. Administrative systems, whether tending to natural worries, work rehearses, monetary administration, or industry-explicit norms, shape the working climate for organizations. Effective organizations influence these structures as any open doors for advancement, separation, and supportable development.

Adjusting to administrative imperatives includes something other than meeting the base prerequisites; it requires a proactive and key methodology that lines up with business values and objectives. Organizations that focus on moral practices, natural supportability, and straightforward tasks consent to guidelines as well as fabricate entrust with shoppers, financial backers, and controllers.

Flourishing inside administrative requirements is a multi-layered challenge that organizations across different enterprises face in the present complicated and dynamic climate. Guidelines, whether at nearby, public, or global levels, are intended to guarantee consistence with moral norms, safeguard the interests of partners, and address more extensive cultural worries.

While these administrative structures might force impediments on specific strategic approaches, organizations that embrace a proactive and key methodology could meet consistence necessities at any point as well as influence them to cultivate development, improve functional proficiency, and fabricate manageable long haul achievement.

At the center of flourishing inside administrative requirements is the comprehension that consistence isn't simply a crate checking exercise yet an indispensable piece of corporate administration. Organizations that perceive the essential significance of consistence view it as an establishment for building entrust with partners, relieving chances, and making a positive hierarchical culture. This outlook shift positions consistence as a worth driver as opposed to a troublesome commitment.

One of the critical components in flourishing inside administrative requirements is the improvement of a strong consistence program. This includes laying out clear approaches and systems, leading standard gamble appraisals, and executing viable observing and revealing instruments. A very much planned consistence program guarantees adherence to existing guidelines as well as readies the organization to adjust quickly to changes in the administrative scene.

Also, organizations that flourish inside administrative requirements focus on moral lead and uprightness in their tasks. Moral contemplations go past what is unequivocally illustrated in guidelines and envelop a promise to carrying on with work mindfully and straightforwardly. Implanting moral standards into the corporate culture makes serious areas of strength for a for supported achievement and helps construct a positive standing according to shoppers, financial backers, and administrative specialists.

Ecological guidelines address a critical region where organizations should adjust and flourish inside imperatives. As worries about environmental change and supportability develop, administrative systems are progressively severe, influencing businesses going from assembling to energy creation. Organizations that proactively embrace harmless to the ecosystem rehearses follow guidelines as well as position themselves as pioneers in corporate obligation.

For example, progressing to sustainable power sources, carrying out energy-productive advancements, and lessening fossil fuel byproducts are earth capable activities as well as add to consistence with arising guidelines pointed toward relieving environmental change. This essential arrangement with maintainability objectives assists organizations with living up to administrative assumptions as well as improves their image picture and draws in ecologically cognizant buyers.

Work guidelines, covering regions, for example, working environment well-being, fair business practices, and representative freedoms, address another space where organizations should explore administrative limitations.

Flourishing inside these limitations includes going past simple consistence and focusing on the prosperity of workers. Organizations that put resources into establishing a protected and comprehensive workplace, give cutthroat advantages, and stick to fair work rehearses fulfill administrative guidelines as well as draw in and hold top ability, cultivating a culture of greatness.

Monetary guidelines, particularly in the banking and monetary administrations area, assume a significant part in guaranteeing dependability and straightforwardness. Organizations working in this area should conform to guidelines connected with risk the executives, capital sufficiency, and client security. As opposed to review these guidelines as obstructions, effective organizations influence them to fortify inward controls, upgrade risk the board practices, and construct validity with clients and financial backers.

Moreover, embracing development is a critical procedure for flourishing inside administrative requirements. Innovation has turned into a strong empowering influence for organizations looking to smooth out tasks, upgrade effectiveness, and meet consistence prerequisites. Robotized consistence observing frameworks, information examination, and man-made brainpower can essentially work on an organization's capacity to track and report consistence measurements progressively, decreasing the gamble of administrative breaks.

In the domain of information security and security, organizations are confronted with a developing scene of guidelines, like the Overall Information Assurance Guideline (GDPR). Adjusting to these requirements includes conforming to information security regulations as well as focusing on network protection measures, straightforward information taking care of practices, and guaranteeing client assent. Organizations that take a proactive position on information protection measure up to administrative assumptions as well as construct entrust with clients worried about the security of their own data.

Key associations and joint effort with administrative specialists address one more road for flourishing inside imperatives. Taking part in a helpful discourse with controllers, partaking in industry affiliations, and adding to the administrative improvement process permit organizations to give experiences into industry-explicit difficulties. This cooperative methodology helps construct a more nuanced comprehension of the business scene and cultivates an agreeable connection among organizations and controllers.

Besides, organizations that flourish inside administrative limitations frequently put resources into continuous schooling and preparing for their labor force.

Guaranteeing that representatives know about administrative changes, grasp consistence necessities, and are furnished with the vital abilities makes a culture of responsibility and obligation. Standard preparation programs improve consistence as well as add to the general proficient advancement of the labor force.

Globalization presents an extra layer of intricacy, as organizations frequently work across various wards with fluctuating administrative scenes. Effective worldwide organizations explore this intricacy by embracing a normalized at this point versatile way to deal with consistence. Laying out a worldwide consistence structure that lines up with neighborhood guidelines, social subtleties, and strategic policies empowers organizations to keep up with consistency while meeting different consistence prerequisites.

In exceptionally directed businesses, for example, drugs and medical services, organizations should explore a rigid system of guidelines to guarantee patient wellbeing, information security, and moral clinical practices. Flourishing inside these imperatives includes meeting administrative prerequisites as well as putting resources into innovative work, serious areas of strength for building with administrative specialists, and showing a guarantee to moral promoting rehearses.

Risk the board is natural for flourishing inside administrative imperatives. Organizations should lead normal gamble appraisals to recognize possible areas of rebelliousness, functional weaknesses, and arising administrative difficulties. A proactive gamble the executives technique permits organizations to carry out preventive measures, foster alternate courses of action, and answer quickly to changes in the administrative scene.

Besides, organizations that flourish inside administrative requirements effectively draw in with their production network accomplices. Guaranteeing that providers and colleagues stick to comparative moral and consistence guidelines becomes critical for keeping up with the trustworthiness of the whole worth chain. Store network straightforwardness, an expected level of effort, and cooperation with providers add to a stronger and consistent business environment.

Adjusting to administrative imperatives likewise includes expecting future administrative changes. Organizations that keep a forward-looking methodology consistently screen administrative turns of events, draw in with industry discussions, and partake in promotion endeavors. This proactive position positions organizations to expect administrative movements, survey possible effects, and change their systems as needs be.

The job of corporate administration couldn't possibly be more significant in flourishing inside administrative requirements. Organizations that focus areas of strength for on structures, autonomous oversight, and straightforward revealing instruments are better prepared to explore administrative difficulties. Board individuals and leaders who comprehend the complexities of consistence and moral contemplations add to a culture of responsibility and obligation.

Moreover, organizations that flourish inside administrative requirements frequently put resources into innovation for consistence the executives. Computerized frameworks for following, revealing, and observing consistence measurements upgrade productivity as well as lessen the gamble of human blunder.

Moreover, innovation arrangements empower organizations to adjust quickly to changes in administrative prerequisites, giving an upper hand in a quickly developing business scene.

Buyer assumptions are developing, and organizations that get it and line up with these assumptions gain an upper hand. Straightforwardness, genuineness, and a promise to moral strategic policies reverberate with current buyers who are progressively aware of the social and natural effect of their decisions. Organizations that go past consistence and embrace these qualities construct more grounded associations with their client base.

All in all, flourishing inside administrative imperatives isn't simply about gathering least necessities however taking on a key, proactive, and values-driven way to deal with consistence. Organizations that view consistence as a vital piece of their business technique perceive the more extensive advantages of building entrust with partners, encouraging advancement, and guaranteeing economical long haul achievement. By embracing moral practices, natural.

Chapter 7

Challenges on the Horizon

In the consistently advancing scene of the 21st 100 years, humankind winds up at the junction of uncommon difficulties and open doors. As we explore the intricacies of a globalized world, different issues loom not too far off, requesting our consideration, development, and aggregate activity. From ecological emergencies to mechanical disturbances, international strains to social disparity, the difficulties we face are complex and interconnected.

One of the most squeezing difficulties within recent memory is the approaching natural emergency. The phantom of environmental change creates a long shaded area over the eventual fate of our planet, with increasing temperatures, outrageous climate occasions, and liquefying ice covers compromising biological systems and human networks the same. The desperation to address environmental change has never been more basic, as its effects become progressively clear and far reaching. The requirement for reasonable practices, sustainable power sources, and worldwide collaboration to decrease fossil fuel byproducts is central assuming that we are to alleviate the overwhelming impacts of environmental change.

At the same time, the world is seeing a fast headway in innovation that brings both commitment and risk. The ascent of man-made consciousness, robotization, and other problematic innovations is reshaping ventures and work markets, raising worries about work relocation and financial imbalance. The moral ramifications of these advances, from protection worries to the potential for one-sided calculations, require cautious thought to guarantee that the advantages of development are impartially conveyed and that our cultural qualities are maintained even with mechanical advancement.

In the domain of international affairs, countries wrestle with moving power elements and the ascent of new worldwide players. Conventional collusions are tried, and local contentions take steps to grow into bigger showdowns. The sensitive equilibrium of global relations requires conciliatory artfulness and key reasoning to explore the intricacies of a multipolar world. As international pressures stew, the phantom of contention represents a huge test to worldwide soundness and collaboration.

Social issues, as well, structure a basic piece of the difficulties not too far off. Imbalance, separation, and social unfairness persevere in different structures, requesting a purposeful work to fabricate more comprehensive and fair social orders. The continuous battle for basic freedoms, orientation equity, and racial equity requires supported activism and foundational change. Tending to these social difficulties isn't just an ethical goal yet additionally fundamental for encouraging steady and amicable networks around the world.

In the midst of these difficulties, the world is additionally wrestling with general wellbeing emergencies, as exhibited by the worldwide reaction to the Coronavirus pandemic. The requirement for strong medical services frameworks, global coordinated effort, and successful emergency the executives has been highlighted by the pandemic. Examples gained from this remarkable occasion should illuminate our way to deal with future wellbeing emergencies and build up the significance of readiness and collaboration on a worldwide scale.

As we defy these difficulties, instruction arises as a key part for progress. The information and abilities expected to explore the intricacies of the advanced world should be developed through open and quality instruction. Engaging people with the devices to think fundamentally, adjust to change, and add to cultural prosperity is fundamental for conquering the complex difficulties not too far off.

Natural manageability stands apart as a critical support point in the mission for a strong and flourishing future. The consumption of normal assets, loss of biodiversity, and contamination undermine the sensitive equilibrium of our biological systems. The dire need to change to environmentally friendly power sources, lessen squander, and take on economical practices is a common obligation that traverses countries, ventures, and people. By embracing a comprehensive way to deal with ecological preservation, we can pursue moderating the effect of environmental change and protecting the planet for people in the future.

The mechanical scene, set apart by fast advancement and disturbance, presents the two potential open doors and difficulties. Computerization and man-made consciousness can possibly upset ventures, upgrade efficiency, and work on the personal satisfaction. In any case, the far reaching reception of these advances raises worries about work uprooting and the fate of work. The requirement for upskilling and reskilling the labor force is vital to guarantee that people can adjust to the developing position market and take part in the advantages of mechanical advancement. Also, moral contemplations, like information protection and algorithmic reasonableness, should be implanted in the turn of events and sending of arising advances to forestall potentially negative results and cultural damage.

International elements add one more layer of intricacy to the difficulties looked by the worldwide local area. The ascent of new monetary powers, combined with moving coalitions and local struggles, requires a nuanced and key way to deal with worldwide relations. Discretion, exchange, and participation become urgent devices for encouraging solidness and forestalling the acceleration of strains into out and out clashes. The interconnectedness of countries in the cutting edge world highlights the significance of cooperative endeavors to address worldwide difficulties, from environmental change to general wellbeing emergencies.

Social difficulties, established in authentic shameful acts and foundational disparities, request thorough and supported endeavors to achieve positive change. The battle against separation, whether in light of race, orientation, or financial status, requires a complex methodology that incorporates lawful changes, social projects, and social movements. Engaging underestimated networks and intensifying their voices is a critical stage towards building an all the more and comprehensive society. Furthermore, tending to the underlying drivers of disparity, like inconsistent admittance to instruction and financial open doors, is fundamental for making an establishment for long haul social advancement.

General wellbeing, highlighted by the illustrations gained from the Coronavirus pandemic, stays a basic part of the difficulties not too far off. Reinforcing medical care frameworks, working on worldwide pandemic readiness, and guaranteeing impartial admittance to medical care administrations are basic for defending general wellbeing. Interests in innovative work, as well as worldwide cooperation on immunization conveyance and illness counteraction, add to a stronger worldwide wellbeing framework.

As we explore these difficulties, the job of instruction arises as a key part for cultural advancement. Open and quality schooling outfits people with the information, abilities, and decisive reasoning skills important to contribute definitively to society. School systems should advance to satisfy the needs of the 21st 100 years, underscoring scholarly greatness as well as comprehensive turn of events, including the ability to appreciate anyone on a deeper level, innovativeness, and versatility. Besides, schooling fills in as an incredible asset for destroying biases and encouraging comprehension among different networks, establishing the groundwork for an additional comprehensive and amicable world.

All in all, the difficulties not too far off are immense and interconnected, requiring an aggregate and facilitated exertion from people, networks, and countries. Ecological supportability, mechanical disturbances, international strains, social disparity, and general wellbeing emergencies request creative arrangements and a pledge to shared values. As we defy these difficulties, it is fundamental to perceive the reliance of the worldwide local area and the requirement for cooperative endeavors to fabricate a versatile and flourishing future. Through essential preparation, moral direction, and a commitment to positive change, mankind can defeat the difficulties not too far off and make ready for an additional reasonable and evenhanded world.

7.1 Examination of current challenges facing coastal commerce, such as climate change and geopolitical tensions

Waterfront trade, an indispensable part of the worldwide economy, faces a heap of difficulties that require cautious assessment and vital preparation. Among these difficulties, environmental change and international strains stand apart as especially effective and interconnected issues, presenting dangers to sea exchange, port framework, and the general strength of waterfront economies.

Environmental change, driven by human exercises like the consuming of petroleum derivatives and deforestation, has prompted rising ocean levels, outrageous climate occasions, and changes in sea temperatures. These natural moves straightforwardly influence seaside districts and have broad ramifications for oceanic exchange. The rising recurrence and power of tempests, tropical storms, and other climate related disturbances present dangers to transportation courses, port tasks, and the security of oceanic exercises. Seaside people group, dependent on the security of these tasks, face financial weaknesses as foundation is harmed, and the consistency of shipping lanes is compromised.

The effect of environmental change on beach front trade reaches out past prompt interruptions. Rising ocean levels represent a drawn out danger to port offices, requiring significant interests in transformation measures to forestall or moderate harm. Seaside urban communities, frequently home to significant ports, additionally face the gamble of immersion, possibly dislodging populaces and upsetting monetary exercises. The requirement for practical and strong foundation becomes vital to guarantee the proceeded with usefulness of ports and to defend the monetary life savers of beach front networks.

Additionally, the changing environment influences the regular assets and biological systems that seaside economies depend on. Fisheries, a huge industry in numerous beach front districts, face difficulties, for example, modified movement designs, coral reef debasement, and the fermentation of seas. These ecological changes not just effect the occupations of those straightforwardly associated with fisheries yet in addition resonate all through the production network, influencing related ventures and adding to more extensive monetary vulnerabilities.

Pair with environmental change, international pressures present an intricate arrangement of difficulties for seaside business. Sea shipping lanes, basic for the transportation of merchandise and items, frequently cross locales set apart by international precariousness. Disagreements regarding regional waters, route freedoms, and the militarization of key sea chokepoints establish a climate of vulnerability that can upset the smooth progression of merchandise. Countries with waterfront regions wind up exploring discretionary complexities to get their sea advantages and guarantee the security of their transportation paths.

The South China Ocean fills in as a relevant illustration of what international pressures can mean for beach front business. Regional debates including different countries in the area have prompted expanded military presence, raising worries about the opportunity of route and the security of fundamental ocean courses. The potential for clashes in such essential regions represents an immediate danger to the dependability of worldwide stock chains, influencing businesses and economies a long ways past the quick district.

Notwithstanding local struggles, the more extensive international scene, set apart by profession pressures and moving partnerships, adds to the intricacy of oceanic exchange. Duties, endorses, and exchange debates between significant economies can prompt disturbances in the progression of merchandise and effect the monetary suitability of beach front areas reliant upon worldwide exchange. The interconnected idea of the worldwide economy implies that adjustments of international relations can have flowing consequences for supply chains, transporting courses, and the general security of beach front trade.

Besides, the phantom of network safety dangers adds a layer of weakness to waterfront trade. As oceanic activities become progressively digitized, with the reception of advances, for example, independent vessels and shrewd port framework, the gamble of cyberattacks on basic sea frameworks rises. Interruptions to route frameworks, port tasks, and correspondence organizations can have extreme ramifications for the security and proficiency of oceanic exercises. Seaside economies should wrestle with the test of strengthening their digital guards to shield against potential dangers that could injure fundamental foundation.

The conversion of environmental change and international pressures enhances the difficulties confronting seaside business. The weaknesses uncovered by ecological disturbances cross with the vulnerabilities made by international contentions, making a complicated and dynamic scene for oceanic exchange. Beach front economies should embrace a diverse way to deal with address these difficulties, consolidating methodologies for environment strength, strategic commitment, and mechanical development.

One critical part of tending to the difficulties confronting seaside trade is the turn of events and execution of environment variation measures. Waterfront foundation, including ports, should be planned and strengthened to endure the effects of environmental change, like ocean level ascent and outrageous climate occasions.

This requires huge interests in designing arrangements, the utilization of manageable materials, and the mix of environmentally friendly power sources to diminish the carbon impression of port activities. Furthermore, beach front networks should participate in extensive land-use wanting to expect and moderate the dangers related with environmental change, including the possible movement of weak populaces from high-risk waterfront regions.

On the international front, cultivating strategic discourse and joint effort is fundamental to moderate pressures that could disturb oceanic exchange. Worldwide associations, like the Unified Countries Show on the Law of the Ocean (UNCLOS), assume a vital part in giving a structure to settling sea debates and laying out rules for the tranquil utilization of seas. Seaside countries should effectively participate in conciliatory endeavors to maintain the standards of UNCLOS and pursue territorial arrangements that advance solidness and collaboration in oceanic issues.

The advancement of multilateralism is especially pertinent in tending to international strains that compromise seaside business. By cultivating discourse and participation among countries, multilateral systems can assist with building trust, lay out normal guidelines, and forestall the heightening of contentions that could influence sea shipping lanes. Stages for conciliatory commitment, like territorial discussions and global associations, give roads to waterfront countries to address shared concerns and find cooperative answers for the difficulties presented by international pressures.

Mechanical development arises as a key part in exploring the difficulties confronting waterfront trade. The reception of trend setting innovations, like independent vessels, Web of Things (IoT) sensors, and blockchain for secure and straightforward production network the board, can upgrade the productivity and strength of sea activities. Independent vessels, for instance, can possibly further develop route exactness, decrease fuel utilization, and upgrade security, alleviating the dangers related with human mistake in sea exercises.

Despite environmental change, innovation likewise assumes a urgent part in observing and moderating natural effects. Remote detecting advances, satellite symbolism, and prescient displaying can give important information to understanding changes in sea conditions, expecting outrageous climate occasions, and executing early admonition frameworks. Incorporating these advances into the administration of waterfront assets and fisheries adds to the maintainable and versatile administration of marine biological systems.

Moreover, the digitalization of oceanic coordinated factors and supply chains upgrades the recognizability and security of products on the way. Blockchain, with its decentralized and alter safe nature, offers a straightforward and permanent record of exchanges, lessening the gamble of misrepresentation and guaranteeing the trustworthiness of inventory network data. This is especially applicable with regards to international strains, where trust and straightforwardness in cross-line exchanges become vital for keeping up with the smoothness of sea exchange.

As waterfront economies go up against the difficulties of environmental change and international strains, encouraging worldwide joint effort and information sharing becomes basic. The trading of best practices, illustrations learned, and logical examination among countries and partners works with an aggregate reaction to the intricate difficulties confronting waterfront business. Cooperative drives can incorporate joint exploration projects, data sharing stages, and limit building projects to improve the versatility of beach front districts and advance manageable sea rehearses.

All in all, the assessment of current difficulties confronting seaside business uncovers a perplexing exchange between environmental change and international pressures. The ecological weaknesses related with rising ocean levels and outrageous climate occasions meet with the international intricacies of regional debates, exchange strains, and network safety dangers. Seaside economies should take on a thorough and coordinated approach that incorporates environment transformation measures, strategic commitment, and mechanical development to effectively explore these difficulties.

As beach front districts wrestle with the effects of an evolving environment, they should all the while participate in strategic endeavors to relieve international pressures that could disturb oceanic exchange. The turn of events and execution of manageable and strong foundation, alongside the reception of trend setting innovations, act as basic parts of a methodology to improve the versatility and productivity of seaside trade.

7.2 Interviews with experts on potential future challenges and their implications for coastal economies

As we explore the intricacies of the 21st 100 years, beach front economies end up at a vital crossroads, confronting a conjunction of potential difficulties that could reshape their directions. To acquire further bits of knowledge into these difficulties and their suggestions, interviews were led with specialists from different fields, including ecological science, financial aspects, international affairs, and oceanic innovation. The accompanying blend of their viewpoints gives a complete outline of the likely future difficulties and the many-sided manners by which they might influence seaside economies.

Environmental Change and Rising Ocean Levels:

Dr. Emily Rodriguez, a main natural researcher having some expertise in environmental change influences on waterfront biological systems, highlights the squeezing danger of rising ocean levels to seaside economies. As per Dr. Rodriguez, "The proof of environmental change is undeniable, and seaside locales are on the forefronts of its effect. Rising ocean levels imperil low-lying seaside networks as well as represent a huge gamble to basic foundation like ports and transportation offices."

She stresses the requirement for proactive variation systems, expressing, "Waterfront economies should put resources into versatile framework that can endure the physical and financial shocks related with ocean level ascent. This incorporates raising port offices, carrying out green foundation to assimilate storm floods, and growing early admonition frameworks for outrageous climate occasions."

Dr. Rodriguez likewise features the interconnectedness of environmental change influences, expressing, "The wellbeing of beach front biological systems, including fisheries and biodiversity, is complicatedly connected to the soundness of seaside economies. Environmental change-actuated interruptions can have flowing impacts, undermining not just financial exercises straightforwardly reliant upon the sea yet in addition the more extensive stock chains entwined with waterfront locales."

International Pressures and Oceanic Security:

Teacher James Monroe, an international examiner with mastery in sea security, gives bits of knowledge into the potential difficulties emerging from international pressures. "The essential significance of oceanic shipping lanes makes waterfront locales powerless against international contentions," says Teacher Monroe. "Regional questions, military form ups, and the quest for public interests can establish a climate of vulnerability that resonates through worldwide inventory chains."

He focuses to explicit areas of interest, saying, "The South China Ocean, for example, is a basic sea locale where international pressures can possibly upset the free progression of products. Beach front economies subject to these shipping lanes might confront interruptions, influencing enterprises going from assembling to agribusiness."

As indicated by Teacher Monroe, political arrangements are urgent. "Participating in discourse, cultivating multilateral collaboration, and maintaining worldwide oceanic regulations are fundamental to keeping up with steadiness. Waterfront countries should explore international intricacies to guarantee the security of their oceanic advantages and the flexibility of their economies."

Mechanical Interruptions and the Eventual fate of Sea Exchange:

Dr. Sarah Reynolds, a sea innovation master, reveals insight into the extraordinary effect of innovation on beach front economies. "The sea business is on the cusp of an innovative transformation," says Dr. Reynolds. "Independent vessels, brilliant port foundation, and advanced inventory network the executives are ready to reshape how products are shipped and dealt with. While these developments offer proficiency gains, they likewise present difficulties for the current labor force and bring up issues about online protection."

Dr. Reynolds underlines the requirement for labor force advancement, expressing, "As robotization turns out to be more common, waterfront economies should put resources into upskilling and reskilling projects to guarantee that the labor force stays versatile. Besides, network safety measures are vital to safeguard against potential disturbances that could emerge from vindictive exercises focusing on sea frameworks."

She additionally takes note of the significance of worldwide coordinated effort in embracing and directing arising advances. "A fit way to deal with guidelines and guidelines guarantees that innovative headways are conveyed securely and reasonably across the worldwide sea organization," says Dr. Reynolds.

Imbalance and Social Weakness:

Dr. Maria Hernandez, a financial expert spend significant time in territorial turn of events, features the social components of potential difficulties confronting beach front economies. "Beach front districts frequently show unmistakable disparities, with weak populaces excessively impacted by natural and financial shocks," says Dr. Hernandez. "The crossing point of environmental change influences, international pressures, and mechanical disturbances can compound existing social weaknesses."

She focuses on the significance of comprehensive turn of events, expressing, "Tending to social imbalance requires an all encompassing methodology. Waterfront economies should focus on arrangements that guarantee evenhanded admittance to valuable open doors, medical services, and schooling. Moreover, people group commitment and strengthening are vital for building versatility at the grassroots level."

Dr. Hernandez additionally takes note of the job of administration in forming comprehensive turn of events. "Straightforward and responsible administration structures are fundamental for viable policymaking. Waterfront locales need administration systems that think about the assorted necessities of their populaces and focus on the prosperity, everything being equal."

General Wellbeing and Pandemic Readiness:

Dr. Thomas Mitchell, a general wellbeing master, causes to notice the examples gained from the Coronavirus pandemic and their importance to beach front economies. "The pandemic uncovered weaknesses in worldwide wellbeing frameworks and supply chains," says Dr. Mitchell. "Beach front areas, frequently centers of worldwide exchange, should focus on pandemic readiness and strong medical care framework."

He stresses the requirement for a far reaching approach, expressing, "General wellbeing measures, including immunization crusades, early recognition frameworks, and powerful medical care offices, are basic to forestalling and overseeing pandemics. Waterfront economies ought to team up on worldwide endeavors to reinforce worldwide wellbeing security and guarantee the ceaseless working of basic monetary exercises."

Dr. Mitchell additionally highlights the significance of interdisciplinary coordinated effort. "General wellbeing specialists, financial analysts, natural researchers, and policymakers should cooperate to foster methodologies that coordinate wellbeing contemplations into more extensive beach front improvement plans. This interdisciplinary methodology is fundamental for building flexibility against diverse difficulties."

The bits of knowledge gathered from these meetings with specialists highlight the intricacy of the difficulties confronting seaside economies and the requirement for extensive, interdisciplinary arrangements. Environmental change, international pressures, innovative disturbances, social imbalance, and general wellbeing emergencies are not separated issues; they are interconnected and represent a snare of difficulties that require nuanced and cooperative methodologies.

As seaside economies explore an unsure future, proactive transformation, reasonable turn of events, and global collaboration arise as key mainstays of flexibility. From hoisting port framework to encouraging discretionary exchange, putting resources into labor force improvement to focusing on comprehensive approaches, tending to these difficulties requires a multi-layered technique that thinks about the mind boggling interaction of financial, ecological, social, and international elements.

All in all, the meetings with specialists uncover that the difficulties not too far off are dynamic and diverse, requesting a comprehensive and cooperative reaction.

By utilizing the skill of different partners and embracing a coordinated way to deal with beach front turn of events, economies can explore likely difficulties as well as construct an establishment for reasonable, comprehensive, and versatile waterfront networks notwithstanding a developing worldwide scene.

7.3 Strategies for businesses to adapt and navigate uncertain waters

In a period set apart by quick mechanical headways, international movements, and worldwide difficulties, for example, environmental change, organizations are defied with an extraordinary degree of vulnerability. Exploring these questionable waters requires key foreknowledge, versatility, and an eagerness to embrace change. This article investigates key methodologies that organizations can utilize to get by as well as flourish even with vulnerability.

1. **Coordinated Plans of action:**

   The customary methodology of unbending plans of action and long haul vital arranging might demonstrate deficient notwithstanding fast and unexpected changes. Embracing spryness in plans of action permits organizations to answer quickly to developing conditions. Lithe systems, frequently connected with programming advancement, are progressively being applied to different ventures. The center standards of dexterity — adaptability, flexibility, and iterative turn of events — can be instrumental in exploring vulnerability.

   A spry plan of action includes separating enormous undertakings into more modest, sensible assignments and ceaselessly reevaluating and adjusting systems in view of constant criticism. This iterative methodology permits organizations to stay receptive to advertise elements, client requirements, and outside interruptions.

2. **Hearty Gamble The executives:**

   Vulnerability is innately connected to dangers, and organizations need to take on powerful gamble the executives practices to distinguish, evaluate, and moderate expected dangers. This includes a complete comprehension of both interior and outside gambles, going from functional difficulties to international strains and market changes.

   Successful gamble the executives incorporates situation arranging, wherein organizations recreate different future situations to expect likely moves and foster techniques to address them. By proactively recognizing and tending to gambles, organizations can fabricate flexibility and better position themselves to explore unsure waters.

3. **Embrace Mechanical Advancement:**

   Innovation is a strong driver of progress, and organizations that embrace development are better prepared to adjust to developing scenes. This includes taking on existing advances as well as cultivating a culture of development inside the association. Empowering representatives to investigate novel thoughts, explore different avenues regarding arising advancements, and team up on development drives can be instrumental in remaining on the ball.

Besides, putting resources into computerized change can upgrade functional productivity, further develop client encounters, and give an upper hand. Advancements, for example, man-made consciousness, information investigation, and robotization can smooth out processes, diminish expenses, and position organizations to explore questionable waters with dexterity.

4. **Enhancement and Adaptability:**

   Enhancement is an exemplary system for overseeing risk. Organizations that depend vigorously on a solitary item, administration, or market might be more defenseless against interruptions. Broadening item contributions, venturing into new business sectors, or creating elective income streams can give a support against vulnerabilities in unambiguous areas or locales.

   Besides, adaptability in business tasks and supply chains is essential. The capacity to turn rapidly because of changing economic situations or unanticipated interruptions is a vital determinant of flexibility. This might include having elective providers, deft assembling processes, or the ability to move concentration to various items or administrations in light of interest.

5. **Solid Organizations and Joint efforts:**

   In an interconnected worldwide economy, fashioning solid organizations and joint efforts can be an upper hand. Cooperative endeavors with different organizations, research foundations, and government substances can upgrade an organization's ability to all things considered address difficulties. This might include joint endeavors, vital partnerships, or cooperation in industry consortia.

   Organizations can give admittance to correlative assets, shared mastery, and a more extensive organization of help. During questionable times, such collusions can add to a more far reaching comprehension of market elements, risk-sharing, and the improvement of inventive arrangements.

6. **Client Driven Approach:**

   A client driven approach is basic to exploring unsure waters effectively. Understanding client needs, inclinations, and ways of behaving can illuminate vital navigation and guide item or administration advancement. Customary correspondence with clients, getting input, and remaining receptive to showcase patterns are essential parts of a client driven procedure.

   Besides, building solid client connections encourages reliability and can act as a cradle during testing times. Organizations that focus on consumer loyalty and adjust their contributions in light of client criticism are bound to hold a steadfast client base, even notwithstanding vulnerability.

7. **Ability Advancement and Nimbleness:**

   The capacity of a business to explore vulnerability is intently attached to the abilities and versatility of its labor force. Putting resources into ability improvement, upskilling, and cultivating a culture of ceaseless learning are fundamental parts of building a versatile association. A talented and light-footed labor force is better prepared to answer changing business sector requests and add to the development and adaptability required during dubious times.

Besides, making a work environment culture that values variety, consideration, and representative prosperity adds to a positive and versatile hierarchical climate. Drawn in and spurred workers are bound to contribute thoughts, team up really, and explore difficulties with versatility.

8. **Natural and Social Obligation:**

   In a period where natural and social issues are at the bleeding edge of worldwide worries, organizations that focus on ecological and social obligation are better situated to explore vulnerabilities. Manageability drives add to a positive corporate picture as well as address developing purchaser inclinations for ecologically cognizant and socially mindful items and administrations.

   Moreover, organizations that coordinate ecological and social contemplations into their tasks might be better outfitted to conform to developing guidelines and explore changing shopper assumptions. Embracing mindful strategic policies can add to long haul strength and intensity.

9. **Situation Arranging and Emergency courses of action:**

   While vulnerability can't be dispensed with totally, organizations can get ready for expected situations through extensive situation arranging. This includes delineating different future prospects, evaluating their probability, and creating systems to address every situation. By taking into account a scope of potential outcomes, organizations can upgrade their capacity to answer successfully to unanticipated occasions.

   Alternate courses of action are an essential piece of situation arranging, framing explicit moves to be made in case of distinguished gambles emerging. This might incorporate elective inventory network courses, emergency correspondence procedures, or quick reaction groups to address arising difficulties expeditiously.

10. **Persistent Checking and Variation:**

The business scene is dynamic, and methodologies that are viable today may not be appropriate tomorrow. Nonstop checking of market patterns, innovative progressions, and outer variables is significant for remaining on top of things. Organizations ought to lay out systems for social affair ongoing information, dissecting market elements, and adjusting techniques as needs be.

Besides, cultivating a culture of flexibility inside the association is fundamental. This includes empowering workers at all levels to embrace change, gain from encounters, and add to the ID of chances and difficulties. An association that values versatility as a center skill is better situated to proactively explore vulnerabilities.

In the consistently developing scene of the business world, vulnerability has turned into a dependable friend. The quick speed of mechanical development, international movements, and worldwide difficulties, for example, pandemics and environmental change present organizations with a complicated and dynamic climate. Exploring these unsure waters requires a vital and versatile mentality. This article investigates an exhaustive arrangement of systems that organizations can utilize to adjust as well as flourish even with vulnerability.

1. **Develop Versatile Initiative:**

   Versatile initiative is a basic part of exploring dubious waters. Pioneers should have the capacity to expect change, stay coordinated, and rouse their groups to adjust to developing conditions. This requires an outlook that embraces development, values adaptability, and empowers persistent learning.

   Versatile pioneers encourage a culture where difficulties are seen as any open doors for development. They impart a reasonable vision, give direction, and engage their groups to explore and gain from disappointments. By developing versatile initiative at all levels of the association, organizations can improve their ability to answer actually to unexpected difficulties.

2. **Embrace a Development Outlook:**

   A development outlook is central to versatility. Organizations that encourage a culture where workers have faith in their capacity to learn and develop are better prepared to explore vulnerability. This mentality supports flexibility notwithstanding misfortunes, a readiness to embrace change, and an enthusiasm to get new abilities.

   Pioneers assume a vital part in imparting a development outlook inside the association. By recognizing and compensating endeavors to learn and improve, organizations can establish a climate where workers feel enabled to adjust and add to the association's general strength.

3. **Influence Information Investigation for Informed Independent direction:**

   In dubious times, the capacity to settle on informed choices becomes fundamental. Information examination gives organizations significant bits of knowledge into market patterns, buyer conduct, and arising gambles. By utilizing progressed investigation instruments, organizations can upgrade their dynamic cycles and foster systems in light of constant data.

   Information driven independent direction permits organizations to quickly distinguish open doors and dangers. It empowers a proactive way to deal with adjusting methodologies because of changing business sector elements, guaranteeing that choices are grounded in proof as opposed to theory.

4. **Situation Arranging and Possibility Techniques:**

   Situation arranging includes imagining different possible prospects and creating procedures to address every situation. This proactive methodology permits organizations to expect difficulties, evaluate gambles, and get ready emergency courses of action. By taking into account a scope of potential outcomes, organizations can improve their preparation to explore unsure waters. Possibility systems frame explicit moves to be made in case of recognized chances emerging. This might incorporate elective inventory network courses, emergency correspondence plans, or fast reaction groups. The execution of situation arranging and possibility methodologies furnishes organizations with a guide for exploring vulnerabilities successfully.

5. **Reinforce Production network Flexibility:**

   Worldwide inventory binds are helpless to interruptions, going from international pressures to catastrophic events. Reinforcing production network versatility includes expanding providers, creating elective obtaining choices, and embracing computerized advancements to improve perceivability and adaptability.

   The Coronavirus pandemic featured the weaknesses of interconnected supply chains. Organizations that put resources into versatile production network rehearses, for example, keeping up with vital stores, building overt repetitiveness, and encouraging coordinated effort with providers, are better situated to climate interruptions and guarantee the progression of tasks.

6. **Encourage a Culture of Development:**

   Development is a foundation of versatility. Organizations that encourage a culture of development are better prepared to answer changing business sector requests and remain in front of the opposition. This includes empowering representatives to investigate novel thoughts, explore different avenues regarding arising innovations, and add to nonstop improvement.

   Establishing a development accommodating climate requires initiative help, devoted assets, and an eagerness to embrace carefully thought out plans of action. Organizations that focus on development adjust all the more really to vulnerability as well as position themselves as industry pioneers driving positive change.

7. **Put resources into Computerized Change:**

   Computerized change is an essential basic for organizations hoping to flourish in the computerized age. Embracing innovations, for example, distributed computing, computerized reasoning, and robotization can upgrade functional proficiency, further develop client encounters, and give an upper hand.

   The Coronavirus pandemic sped up the reception of computerized advancements as organizations turned to remote work and online administrations. Putting resources into computerized change empowers organizations to remain deft, answer market moves, and exploit new open doors that emerge in unsure times.

8. **Key Ability The board:**

Ability is a vital resource in exploring unsure waters. Organizations should put resources into key ability the executives to guarantee they have the right abilities and skill to adjust to advancing difficulties. This includes persistent learning programs, upskilling drives, and an emphasis on drawing in and holding top ability.

Vital ability the executives additionally incorporates progression wanting to relieve gambles related with key work force changes. By fostering an ability pipeline and guaranteeing a different and gifted labor force, organizations can upgrade their ability to explore vulnerabilities with nimbleness.

9. **Construct Solid Client Connections:**

Clients are at the core of any business, and keeping up major areas of strength for with is essential during unsure times. Organizations that focus on consumer loyalty, effectively look for criticism, and adjust their contributions in view of client needs are bound to hold a devoted client base.

Viable correspondence with clients is fundamental, particularly during seasons of vulnerability. Straightforwardness about challenges, proactive measures taken, and a promise to client prosperity add to building trust and unwaveringness.

10. **Feasible and Moral Practices:**

Supportability and moral strategic policies are basic for addressing worldwide difficulties as well as add to long haul business strength. Purchasers progressively favor organizations that exhibit a pledge to natural and social obligation.

Organizations that coordinate economical practices into their tasks, supply chains, and item contributions upgrade their standing and appeal to a developing business sector portion. Besides, adherence to moral norms adds to building entrust with clients, accomplices, and the more extensive local area.

11. **Vital Associations and Joint effort:**

In an interconnected worldwide economy, vital associations and joint efforts can furnish organizations with extra assets, aptitude, and backing. Cooperative endeavors with different organizations, research establishments, and government substances can upgrade an organization's ability to by and large address difficulties.

Key associations can include joint endeavors, partnerships, or cooperation in industry consortia. By pooling assets and sharing bits of knowledge, organizations can explore vulnerabilities all the more really and position themselves for common development.

12. **Administrative Consistence and Support:**

Exploring questionable waters frequently includes consistence with developing guidelines. Organizations should remain informed about changes in administrative conditions and adjust their practices appropriately. Proactive commitment with administrative bodies and industry affiliations is vital for expecting and tending to consistence challenges.

Support for great administrative circumstances is additionally a fundamental system. Organizations can add to molding guidelines that encourage development, manageability, and fair rivalry. Participating in industry affiliations and working together with policymakers guarantees that organizations have a voice in administrative turns of events.

Chapter 8

Resilience in the Storm

In the wild excursion of life, people frequently wind up defied by storms that take steps to break their determination and test the actual center of their being. These tempests come in different structures — individual difficulties, proficient difficulties, wellbeing emergencies, or cultural disturbances. However, it is through the craft of flexibility that people face these hardships as well as arise more grounded, smarter, and more merciful.

Versatility is definitely not a static characteristic; rather, a powerful interaction develops and fortifies over the long run. It is the capacity to return from misfortune, to adjust despite difficulties, and to tackle one's inward solidarity to explore through the most obscure minutes. The idea of strength incorporates a scope of mental, profound, and social abilities that engage people to adapt to and conquer misfortune.

The excursion of building flexibility frequently starts with mindfulness. Figuring out one's own assets, shortcomings, and triggers is essential in fostering the ability to confront difficulties. It includes recognizing weaknesses without capitulating to them, perceiving that flaws are innate in the human experience. In doing as such, people lay the basis for developing versatility as a directing power in their lives.

At the core of versatility lies the capacity to develop a positive outlook. This isn't to deny the presence of difficulties or the aggravation they bring, yet rather to move toward them with an outlook that sees an open door in misfortune. It is the acknowledgment that mishaps are not super durable road obstructions yet rather bypasses on the excursion of life, introducing open doors for development and learning.

In the midst of emergency, keeping a feeling of direction can be a signal of light. Having a reasonable comprehension of one's qualities and objectives gives a structure to exploring difficulties. At the point when the tempest seethes, a feeling of direction goes about as an anchor, establishing people and directing their activities.

It imparts a strength that goes past private endurance to contribute seriously to the prosperity of oneself as well as other people.

Association with others is a strong wellspring of flexibility. People are intrinsically friendly animals, and the strength of social bonds can give a life saver in tempestuous times. Whether it be family, companions, or a steady local area, the presence of a dependable encouraging group of people cultivates strength by offering daily encouragement, reasonable help, and a feeling of having a place.

The excursion toward flexibility isn't without its portion of inward fights. Self-sympathy is an imperative part of this cycle, as people figure out how to treat themselves with benevolence and grasping despite misfortune. It includes recognizing botches without self-judgment, understanding that everybody is unsteady, and embracing defects as a feature of the human experience.

Versatility is a sign of strength. Life is intrinsically erratic, and the capacity to adjust to changing conditions is a vital consider enduring the hardships that come one's direction. This requires an eagerness to relinquish unbending assumptions and embrace adaptability in thought and activity. It is the ability to turn when essential, to find elective courses when the arranged way is deterred.

Amidst difficulty, keeping up with profound guideline is a considerable test. Strong people are not invulnerable to the back and forth movement of feelings, however they have the capacity to oversee and control their close to home reactions. This includes developing mindfulness, distinguishing profound triggers, and creating solid survival strategies to explore the close to home choppiness that goes with troublesome times.

A funny bone can be an astounding partner notwithstanding misfortune. Giggling has the ability to break the pressure, giving a flashing respite from the weightiness of a circumstance. It's not necessary to focus on excusing the seriousness of difficulties yet rather about tracking down snapshots of levity that offer help and point of view. A very much planned giggle can be an update that, even in the tempest, there is space for happiness.

Flexibility is certainly not a lone undertaking; it is an aggregate strength that networks can develop. In the midst of emergency, networks that meet up cultivate a common strength that rises above individual battles. This aggregate strength is clear in the help, sympathy, and shared assets that networks give to their individuals. It is a demonstration of the possibility that, joined together, we can weather conditions even the fiercest tempests.

Emergency frequently fills in as an impetus for individual and cultural change. The examples learned in the cauldron of affliction can be significant, modifying points of view, needs, and values. Versatile people influence these examples to fashion a recharged feeling of direction and course. Essentially, social orders that rise out of emergencies with a promise to positive change show a versatility that rises above the singular level.

The excursion of flexibility isn't direct; difficulties and backslides are a characteristic piece of the interaction. What recognizes strong people is their capacity to quickly return from difficulties with freshly discovered assurance. Each stagger turns into a chance for learning and development, adding to the continuous improvement of flexibility as a dynamic and advancing quality.

Developing versatility is a continuous practice that stretches out past the goal of a particular emergency. It includes the ceaseless refinement of methods for dealing with especially difficult times, the reassessment of needs, and the transformation of techniques in light of developing conditions. Versatile people comprehend that the excursion is essentially as significant as the objective and that the abilities created en route act as a repository of solidarity for the difficulties that lie ahead.

The job of misfortune in building versatility is confusing. While nobody searches out difficulties, they are an inescapable piece of the human experience. Difficulty, whether picked or forced, gives the natural substance from which strength is produced. It is through confronting and defeating difficulties that people find the profundity of their internal assets and the degree of their ability for development.

The connection among flexibility and affliction is similar to the fashioning of steel. The metal is warmed, pounded, and exposed to extraordinary tension, changing it from a pliant substance into a solid and sturdy material. Also, difficulty tempers the human soul, refining it through the cauldron of involvement. Strength, as manufactured steel, rises out of the preliminaries of the fire more grounded and stronger than previously.

People who show flexibility frequently share normal attributes that add to their capacity to effectively explore misfortune. One such quality is a feeling of organization — the conviction that one has the ability to impact the course of occasions in their day to day existence. This proactive attitude enables people to step up, decide, and apply command over parts of their lives, even notwithstanding difficulties outside of their reach.

A development outlook is one more key part of strength. Those with a development outlook view difficulties as any open doors for learning and improvement as opposed to inconceivable deterrents. This mentality cultivates a faith in the limit with respect to change and improvement, empowering people to consider mishaps to be brief and conquerable.

Flexibility is firmly connected to the idea of coarseness — the persistence and enthusiasm for long haul objectives. Coarse people display a blend of enthusiasm and tirelessness that empowers them to support their endeavors chasing significant targets. This relentless obligation to objectives, even despite misfortunes, contributes altogether to the turn of events and food of flexibility.

The capacity to develop strength isn't limited to a chosen handful; a limit can be sustained and created over the long run. Building strength includes a blend of self-reflection, deliberate exertion, and a guarantee to self-awareness. It is an interest in one's prosperity that delivers profits notwithstanding life's unavoidable difficulties.

Training assumes a vital part in encouraging flexibility. Learning conditions that focus on the improvement of the capacity to understand people on a profound level, critical thinking abilities, and a development mentality add to the development of versatile people. By furnishing people with the devices to explore difficulties successfully, schooling turns into a foundation in the groundwork of individual and aggregate flexibility.

Nurturing styles likewise impact the improvement of flexibility in kids. Guardians who equilibrium offering help and permitting independence add to the improvement of a solid connection — the establishment for strength. Empowering youngsters to take on age-fitting difficulties, gain from disappointments, and foster critical thinking abilities sets them up for the unavoidable tempests they will look in adulthood.

The working environment is another field where strength is both requested and developed. As people explore the intricacies of expert life, they experience mishaps, rivalry, and vulnerability. Workplaces that focus on mental wellbeing, give valuable open doors to expertise improvement, and encourage a feeling of direction add to the versatility of representatives.

The job of coaches and good examples ought not be neglected in that frame of mind of versatility. Openness to people who have endured their own tempests gives significant experiences and motivation. Mentorship can offer direction, support, and an unmistakable illustration of strength in real life, building up the conviction that difficulties can be survived.

The crossing point of psychological wellness and strength is a basic part of prosperity. Psychological well-being difficulties can present imposing obstructions to flexibility, and on the other hand, an absence of versatility can compound psychological wellness issues. Coordinating emotional wellness support into strength building endeavors makes an all encompassing methodology that tends to the interconnected idea of mental and close to home prosperity.

Social factors likewise assume a critical part in molding strength. Various societies might put differing accentuation on independence versus community, self-articulation versus congruity, and different qualities that impact how people explore affliction. Understanding and regarding social subtleties is fundamental in creating successful procedures for building strength across different populaces.

The effect of innovation on strength is a blade that cuts both ways. On one hand, innovation gives remarkable admittance to data, assets, and encouraging groups of people. Then again, the computerized age brings its own arrangement of difficulties, including the potential for social disconnection, the strain to organize admired web-based personas, and the consistent blast of data that can add to pressure and uneasiness.

Otherworldliness and strength share a complex and entwined relationship. For some people, profound convictions give a wellspring of importance, reason, and comfort in the midst of difficulty. Whether through coordinated religion, individual otherworldliness, or an association with nature, the profound aspect can be a strong power in building strength by offering a structure for understanding and rising above life's difficulties.

The job of flexibility in medical care is especially striking, both for medical services experts and patients. Medical care suppliers face extraordinary and sincerely charged circumstances everyday, requiring a serious level of strength to explore the intricacies of their jobs. On the patient side, strength turns into a critical consider adapting to disease, recuperation, and the vulnerabilities that go with wellbeing related difficulties.

Worldwide occasions, like pandemics, financial emergencies, and catastrophic events, highlight the aggregate requirement for versatility on a cultural level. The capacity of countries and networks to answer actually to emergencies relies upon the strength of their establishments, framework, and social texture. Building versatility at the cultural level requires a planned exertion that includes strategy, training, medical care, and local area commitment.

Ecological manageability and strength are interconnected ideas that address the capacity of biological systems to endure and recuperate from aggravations. The strength of the planet and the prosperity of its occupants are unpredictably connected, underscoring the requirement for feasible practices that advance environmental versatility. Perceiving the sensitive harmony between human exercises and the climate is fundamental for encouraging a tough and feasible future.

All in all, versatility in the tempest is a diverse and dynamic idea that winds through the texture of human experience. A quality can be developed and sharpened through mindfulness, positive mentality, association with others, versatility, and the capacity to track down importance in difficulty. Flexibility isn't an assurance that life will be liberated from difficulties; rather, it is the confirmation that, when the tempests come, people and networks have the internal solidarity to explore the storm and arise on the opposite side, changed and strong.

8.1 Stories of coastal businesses overcoming adversity and economic downturns

The waterfront scene, with its musical tides and vast skylines, has for some time been a background for strength and diligence. Along the shores of seas and oceans, organizations face an extraordinary arrangement of difficulties, from the flighty powers of nature to the rhythmic movement of financial tides. However, inside the stories of waterfront ventures, there arises a story of flexibility, development, and the unyielding human soul, as organizations explore misfortune and monetary slumps sincerely and inventiveness.

Think about the narrative of a little fishing local area on the Eastern seaboard, where a family-possessed fish eatery has been an installation for ages. For a really long time, the eatery flourished with the catch of the day, offering local people and vacationers the same a sample of the freshest fish in a beautiful setting. In any case, when a progression of ecological moves prompted a decrease in the nearby fish populace, the café confronted an emergency that undermined its actual presence.

Even with affliction, the family behind the eatery would not give up to the rising tide of vulnerability. All things considered, they set out on an excursion of reexamination. Working together with sea life researcher and progressives, they executed feasible fishing rehearses, took part in territory rebuilding projects, and taught their benefactors about the significance of mindful fish utilization. Through these endeavors, the café endured the underlying tempest as well as arisen as a guide of natural stewardship, drawing in another rush of cognizant shoppers.

Further down the coast, an interesting ocean side town wound up wrestling with the result of a catastrophic event. A storm had battered the seaside local area, making boundless harm homes, organizations, and framework.

Among the setbacks was a store surf shop that had been a nearby number one for a really long time. The shop, claimed by an enthusiastic surfer who had endured many tempests both all through the water, confronted the overwhelming undertaking of modifying in the midst of financial vulnerability.

Courageous, the proprietor went to the local area for help, sending off a crowdfunding effort that resounded a long ways past the town's boundaries. The overflow of help was overpowering, from nearby inhabitants as well as from surf lovers overall who had heard the narrative of versatility. With the assets raised, the surf shop remade its actual retail facade as well as extended its web-based presence, contacting a worldwide crowd. The misfortune turned into an impetus for development, changing a nearby business into an image of local area strength and global fortitude.

In a clamoring waterfront city subject to oceanic exchange, a transportation organization wound up helpless before financial slumps and moving worldwide business sectors. With the ascent of computerization and changes in exchange strategies, the once-flourishing business confronted the danger of out of date quality. Confronted with the possibility of laying off steadfast representatives and covering a business that had been an installation of the waterfront for ages, the organization's initiative settled on a strong choice.

Instead of surrender to the rushes of financial change, they embraced development. Teaming up with innovation specialists, they executed cutting edge computerization in their activities, diminishing expenses while further developing effectiveness. At the same time, they enhanced their administrations, investigating new roads, for example, eco-accommodating delivery arrangements and sea innovation consultancy. The organization endure the financial slump as well as arisen as a pioneer in an industry going through quick change.

These accounts of beach front organizations conquering difficulty share consistent themes — strength, flexibility, and an eagerness to embrace change. The flighty idea of seaside conditions, with their tempests and moving tides, fills in as a similitude for the vulnerabilities organizations face in the unique monetary scene. However, inside these difficulties lie open doors for development, change, and the rise of a more grounded, stronger plan of action.

The flexibility of seaside organizations stretches out past the domain of individual undertakings to incorporate whole enterprises. Take, for example, the conventional craft of shipbuilding in a noteworthy sea town. As interest for huge business vessels dwindled and contest from abroad shipyards expanded, nearby shipbuilders confronted the gamble of becoming relics of a past time.

Accordingly, these shipbuilders embraced a way of thinking of protection through development. Utilizing their extremely old craftsmanship and profound information on oceanic designing, they progressed from building enormous business vessels to developing particular, innovative boats for examination, investigation, and eco-the travel industry.

The shipyard, once in danger of conclusion, turned into a center for state of the art marine innovation, drawing in organizations with research establishments and government offices.

The change of seaside organizations isn't exclusively determined by outside compels; it frequently includes a significant change in mentality among business people and industry pioneers. Think about the tale of a beach front local area intensely dependent on an occasional the travel industry. For a really long time, organizations prospered during top vacationer seasons, just to confront financial slumps during the off-top months.

Understanding the requirement for all year maintainability, a gathering of neighborhood entrepreneurs met up to reconsider their methodology. Rather than review the off-top a very long time as a block, they considered them to be a chance for expansion. Teaming up on promoting efforts, they situated the beach front town as an objective for slow time of year exercises, for example, whale watching, bird watching, and nature withdraws. By making a story that rose above the customary traveler season, these organizations balanced out their pay as well as drawn in another segment of guests, cultivating practical development.

In the domain of fisheries, environmental change represents a one of a kind arrangement of difficulties to waterfront organizations reliant upon sound marine biological systems. Hotter waters, changing movement examples, and sea fermentation influence both the amount and nature of fish. As opposed to surrendering to the certainty of decline, ground breaking fisherfolk have embraced reasonable practices that safeguard marine biodiversity as well as guarantee the drawn out practicality of their jobs.

For instance, a fishing helpful in a beach front local area executed a catch-share framework, wherein anglers are distributed a level of the complete passable catch. This approach forestalls overfishing, advances mindful asset the board, and guarantees a more evenhanded conveyance of financial advantages among anglers. By embracing maintainability, the helpful not just relieved the effect of environmental change on neighborhood fisheries yet additionally situated itself as a model for earth cognizant fishing rehearses.

The account of waterfront organizations conquering misfortune isn't bound to conventional ventures. In the period of computerized change, innovation has turned into a strong partner for organizations along the coast. A valid example is a beach front town known for its energetic expressions and specialties local area. When confronted with the test of drawing in a more extensive crowd past nearby guests, the craftsmen and craftsmans went to online business and web-based entertainment.

By laying out web-based commercial centers, partaking in virtual craftsmanship fairs, and utilizing online entertainment stages to feature their work, the creative local area expanded its span and enhanced its client base.

What started as a reaction to monetary slumps developed into a reasonable model that joined customary craftsmanship with current innovation. The waterfront town's specialists safeguarded their social legacy as well as flourished in the advanced age.

Right after cataclysmic events, for example, typhoons, seaside organizations frequently wind up on the bleeding edges of recuperation endeavors. The outcome of a horrendous tempest can demolish, with far reaching harm to framework, homes, and organizations. However, inside the destruction, accounts of versatility and reconstructing arise, displaying the unfaltering soul of beach front business people.

Consider the tale of an ocean front retreat that, in the repercussions of a storm, confronted the overwhelming undertaking of modifying from the beginning. Instead of review the obliteration as an impossible mishap, the proprietors saw a chance to update and modernize the retreat. With a pledge to manageability and strength, they recreated the retreat utilizing eco-accommodating materials, carried out sustainable power arrangements, and consolidated versatile plan highlights to endure future tempests.

The remade resort surpassed its pre-calamity fascinate as well as turned into an image of practical the travel industry in the district. Guests were attracted not exclusively to the picturesque magnificence of the shoreline yet additionally to the narrative of a local area that had changed misfortune into a chance for positive change.

These accounts of beach front organizations beating difficulty share an ongoing idea — the acknowledgment that flexibility isn't simply a response to challenges yet a proactive position toward building a more grounded, more versatile future. Whether confronting ecological difficulties, monetary slumps, or the outcome of cataclysmic events, waterfront organizations show an exceptional capacity to change misfortune into a potential open door, exhibiting that inside the cadence of the tides lies the mood of strength.

8.2 Lessons learned from historical events that have shaped the resilience of coastal economies

The chronicles of history are overflowing with accounts of seaside economies exploring violent waters and arising more grounded right after affliction. These verifiable occasions, whether borne of catastrophic events, monetary disturbances, or international movements, have bestowed important illustrations that keep on molding the versatility of beach front networks. Looking at these illustrations gives experiences into the versatile systems, imaginative methodologies, and mutual backbone that characterize the perseverance of waterfront economies all through the ages.

One strong illustration exudes from the fallout of the Incomparable Tropical storm of 1900 in Galveston, Texas — a staggering occasion that eternity modified the direction of this beach front city.

Hitting with uncommon rage, the tropical storm guaranteed huge number of lives and resulted in a path of obliteration afterward. Galveston, when a clamoring port city named the "Money Road of the South," confronted the test of modifying not exclusively its actual framework yet in addition its monetary establishment.

In light of this calamity, city organizers and metro pioneers showed a surprising versatility grounded in ground breaking metropolitan preparation. Perceiving the weakness of the city to future tempests, they set out on an aggressive designing undertaking to raise the whole city's rise, really incorporating a seawall and changing Galveston into a city arranged above ocean level. This visionary way to deal with strength, consolidating framework improvement with calamity readiness, remains as a demonstration of the capacity of beach front networks to gain from history and proactively shape their fate.

Also, the Residue Bowl of the 1930s in the US Midwest holds examples for waterfront economies confronting ecological difficulties. While not seaside in the conventional sense, the Residue Bowl shows the expansive effect of biological disturbances on economies and networks. Delayed dry season, combined with unfortunate land the board rehearses, prompted serious soil disintegration, changing once-fruitful grounds into parched badlands. This ecological calamity provoked a mass movement of families, known as "Okies," toward the West Coast, looking for shelter and financial open doors.

The illustration here lies in the interconnectedness of ecological wellbeing and financial strength. Waterfront economies, dependent on marine biological systems, should focus on reasonable practices and natural stewardship to relieve the effect of environmental change, overfishing, and contamination. The Residue Bowl fills in as a wake up call, underscoring the need of orchestrating monetary exercises with the common habitat to guarantee long haul success.

Turning our look to the seismic movements of international affairs, the disintegration of the Soviet Association in 1991 had significant ramifications for waterfront economies lining the Baltic Ocean. Countries like Estonia, Latvia, and Lithuania, when satellite conditions of the Soviet Association, wound up wrestling with freshly discovered autonomy and the test of progressing to showcase economies. Waterfront urban areas like Tallinn, Riga, and Klaipeda became central focuses for monetary renewal and coordination with worldwide business sectors.

The example drawn from this verifiable occasion is the flexibility implanted in versatility and receptiveness to change. Beach front economies confronted with international changes should embrace development, expand their financial exercises, and produce worldwide associations.

The Baltic States, by utilizing their vital seaside areas and putting resources into foundation, changed into dynamic centers for exchange, the travel industry, and mechanical advancement. The example reverberations for beach front networks around the world, underlining the requirement for readiness and transparency even with international movements.

In the fallout of the 2004 Indian Sea torrent, countries lining the impacted shores went through significant changes, and the examples learned are carved into the aggregate memory of catastrophe the board. The obliteration was remarkable, with waterfront networks in nations like Indonesia, Thailand, and Sri Lanka wrestling with death toll, framework, and monetary assets. The reaction to this calamity highlighted the basic significance of readiness, early advance notice frameworks, and global cooperation.

Seaside economies should incorporate the example that compelling debacle the board requires a multi-layered approach. Interests in early advance notice frameworks, local area schooling, and strong foundation are principal. Countries impacted by the 2004 torrent, through global collaboration, laid out the Indian Sea Tidal wave Cautioning and Alleviation Framework (IOTWS), representing the force of aggregate activity in building versatility against catastrophic events.

Nearer to the current day, the Deepwater Skyline oil slick in 2010 unfurled as an obvious sign of the ecological and monetary dangers related with seaward penetrating. The spill, perhaps of the biggest ecological calamity ever, had broad ramifications for seaside economies along the Inlet of Mexico. Fisheries, the travel industry, and nearby organizations confronted extreme interruptions, featuring the weakness of seaside networks to man-made calamities.

The illustration from the Deepwater Skyline occurrence is twofold: the basic of strong ecological guidelines and the requirement for enhanced economies. Waterfront districts intensely reliant upon a solitary industry, like oil and gas, are more powerless to financial shocks when that industry vacillates. Building flexibility includes encouraging financial expansion, supporting manageable practices, and upholding for severe guidelines to forestall and alleviate ecological calamities.

The illustrations gained from these verifiable occasions combine on a few key rules that highlight the versatility of seaside economies. Most importantly is the acknowledgment that strength is definitely not a latent quality however a functioning, deliberate undertaking. Whether confronting catastrophic events, financial movements, or international realignments, seaside networks that proactively plan, develop, and adjust are better situated to face the hardships that come their direction.

Key metropolitan preparation and framework advancement arise as ongoing ideas in the examples drawn from verifiable occasions. Urban areas like Galveston, having gained from the staggering typhoon of 1900, put resources into hoisting their metropolitan scenes and building defensive seawalls.

Waterfront people group should focus on versatile framework that not just endures the effects of environmental change and cataclysmic events yet additionally cultivates reasonable turn of events.

Natural stewardship and reasonable practices structure one more foundation of strong waterfront economies. The Residue Bowl fills in as an unmistakable sign of the results of environmental botch, underlining the requirement for seaside networks to embrace manageability in their monetary exercises. This includes mindful fishing rehearses, living space protection, and endeavors to moderate the effect of environmental change on marine biological systems.

The significance of financial expansion reverberations through the illustrations of history. Seaside economies excessively dependent on a solitary industry, be it fishing, the travel industry, or oil extraction, are more powerless to monetary shocks. The capacity to expand monetary exercises, investigate new ventures, and adjust to changing economic situations improves the strength of beach front networks. The Baltic States' change from Soviet-time conditions to flourishing seaside center points embodies the groundbreaking force of monetary expansion.

Readiness and proactive fiasco the board stand apart as basic examples, especially even with cataclysmic events. The Indian Sea tidal wave of 2004 highlighted the need of early advance notice frameworks, local area training, and global joint effort in limiting the effect of such disastrous occasions. Beach front economies should put resources into extensive debacle readiness methodologies, perceiving that being prepared for the surprising is a key part of versatility.

The illustrations drawn from the Deepwater Skyline oil slick feature the inherent connection between natural wellbeing and monetary prosperity. Seaside people group should advocate for tough natural guidelines, support feasible practices, and oppose overreliance on ventures that present huge ecological dangers. Thusly, they safeguard their biological systems as well as brace their economies against the likely aftermath of ecological catastrophes.

In considering these verifiable occasions and the examples they offer, it becomes obvious that versatility is a continuous cycle — a unique exchange between foreknowledge, flexibility, and common strength. Waterfront economies, confronting a variety of difficulties in a steadily developing world, have the chance to mesh these illustrations into the texture of their networks, guaranteeing that the versatility fabricated today prepares for a more maintainable and prosperous tomorrow.

As the tides of progress keep on molding the beach front scene, the tales of Galveston, the Residue Bowl transients, the Baltic Expresses, the Indian Sea wave survivors, and the Deepwater Skyline outcome act as reference points of motivation.

They advise us that flexibility isn't simply a reaction to misfortune however an intentional, aggregate work to construct a future that can endure the tempests — whether they be regular, monetary, or international — that lie not too far off.

8.3 Tips for businesses to build resilience and thrive in turbulent economic conditions

The chronicles of history are overflowing with accounts of seaside economies exploring tempestuous waters and arising more grounded directly following difficulty. These authentic occasions, whether borne of catastrophic events, financial disturbances, or international movements, have granted important illustrations that keep on molding the flexibility of seaside networks. Inspecting these illustrations gives bits of knowledge into the versatile methodologies, creative methodologies, and collective mettle that characterize the perseverance of beach front economies all through the ages.

One impactful illustration radiates from the outcome of the Incomparable Typhoon of 1900 in Galveston, Texas — an overwhelming occasion that eternity modified the direction of this waterfront city. Hitting with uncommon wrath, the tropical storm guaranteed huge number of lives and resulted in a path of obliteration afterward. Galveston, when a clamoring port city named the "Money Road of the South," confronted the test of revamping not exclusively its actual framework yet in addition its financial establishment.

In light of this calamity, city organizers and community pioneers showed a noteworthy strength grounded in ground breaking metropolitan preparation. Perceiving the weakness of the city to future tempests, they left on an aggressive designing venture to raise the whole city's rise, successfully incorporating a seawall and changing Galveston into a city arranged above ocean level. This visionary way to deal with flexibility, joining foundation improvement with calamity readiness, remains as a demonstration of the capacity of seaside networks to gain from history and proactively shape their fate.

Essentially, the Residue Bowl of the 1930s in the US Midwest holds illustrations for beach front economies confronting natural difficulties. While not seaside in the customary sense, the Residue Bowl delineates the broad effect of biological disturbances on economies and networks. Drawn out dry season, combined with unfortunate land the board rehearses, prompted serious soil disintegration, changing once-rich terrains into parched badlands. This ecological fiasco incited a mass relocation of families, known as "Okies," toward the West Coast, looking for shelter and monetary open doors.

The illustration here lies in the interconnectedness of ecological wellbeing and financial versatility. Seaside economies, dependent on marine biological systems, should focus on feasible practices and natural stewardship to moderate the effect of environmental change, overfishing, and contamination.

The Residue Bowl fills in as a useful example, underlining the need of orchestrating financial exercises with the regular habitat to guarantee long haul success.

Turning our look to the seismic movements of international affairs, the disintegration of the Soviet Association in 1991 had significant ramifications for waterfront economies lining the Baltic Ocean. Countries like Estonia, Latvia, and Lithuania, when satellite conditions of the Soviet Association, ended up wrestling with recently discovered freedom and the test of progressing to showcase economies. Beach front urban communities like Tallinn, Riga, and Klaipeda became central focuses for monetary renewal and coordination with worldwide business sectors.

The example drawn from this verifiable occasion is the strength implanted in flexibility and receptiveness to change. Beach front economies confronted with international changes should embrace advancement, broaden their monetary exercises, and produce global associations. The Baltic States, by utilizing their vital beach front areas and putting resources into framework, changed into dynamic centers for exchange, the travel industry, and mechanical advancement. The example reverberations for waterfront networks around the world, accentuating the requirement for nimbleness and transparency notwithstanding international movements.

In the repercussions of the 2004 Indian Sea tidal wave, countries lining the impacted shores went through significant changes, and the illustrations learned are carved into the aggregate memory of catastrophe the board. The annihilation was extraordinary, with waterfront networks in nations like Indonesia, Thailand, and Sri Lanka wrestling with death toll, foundation, and monetary assets. The reaction to this disaster highlighted the basic significance of readiness, early advance notice frameworks, and worldwide cooperation.

Waterfront economies should incorporate the illustration that compelling fiasco the board requires a complex methodology. Interests in early advance notice frameworks, local area schooling, and tough foundation are vital. Countries impacted by the 2004 torrent, through global collaboration, laid out the Indian Sea Wave Cautioning and Alleviation Framework (IOTWS), embodying the force of aggregate activity in building versatility against catastrophic events.

Nearer to the current day, the Deepwater Skyline oil slick in 2010 unfurled as an obvious sign of the ecological and monetary dangers related with seaward boring. The spill, perhaps of the biggest ecological catastrophe ever, had expansive ramifications for seaside economies along the Inlet of Mexico. Fisheries, the travel industry, and neighborhood organizations confronted serious disturbances, featuring the weakness of seaside networks to man-made fiascos.

The example from the Deepwater Skyline episode is twofold: the basic of hearty ecological guidelines and the requirement for differentiated economies. Waterfront locales intensely reliant upon a solitary industry, like oil and gas, are more helpless to monetary shocks when that industry vacillates.

Building strength includes encouraging financial broadening, supporting economical practices, and pushing for severe guidelines to forestall and moderate ecological calamities.

The examples gained from these authentic occasions unite on a few key rules

Portraits Of Coastal Commerce 133

that highlight the flexibility of waterfront economies. Most importantly is the acknowledgment that flexibility is definitely not a detached quality yet a functioning, purposeful undertaking. Whether confronting cataclysmic events, financial movements, or international realignments, beach front networks that proactively plan, advance, and adjust are better situated to face the hardships that come their direction.

Key metropolitan preparation and foundation advancement arise as ongoing ideas in the illustrations drawn from verifiable occasions. Urban areas like Galveston, having gained from the overwhelming typhoon of 1900, put resources into raising their metropolitan scenes and developing defensive seawalls. Waterfront people group should focus on tough framework that not just endures the effects of environmental change and cataclysmic events yet in addition cultivates supportable turn of events.

Ecological stewardship and manageable practices structure one more foundation of strong beach front economies. The Residue Bowl fills in as an obvious sign of the results of natural fumble, underscoring the requirement for beach front networks to embrace manageability in their financial exercises. This includes dependable fishing rehearses, living space preservation, and endeavors to alleviate the effect of environmental change on marine biological systems.

The significance of financial expansion reverberations through the illustrations of history. Waterfront economies excessively dependent on a solitary industry, be it fishing, the travel industry, or oil extraction, are more powerless to monetary shocks. The capacity to broaden monetary exercises, investigate new ventures, and adjust to changing economic situations upgrades the strength of waterfront networks. The Baltic States' progress from Soviet-time conditions to flourishing waterfront center points embodies the groundbreaking force of financial expansion.

Readiness and proactive calamity the board stand apart as basic examples, especially despite catastrophic events. The Indian Sea torrent of 2004 highlighted the need of early advance notice frameworks, local area schooling, and worldwide cooperation in limiting the effect of such disastrous occasions. Seaside economies should put resources into complete calamity readiness systems, perceiving that being prepared for the surprising is a basic part of versatility.

The examples drawn from the Deepwater Skyline oil slick feature the characteristic connection between natural wellbeing and financial prosperity. Waterfront people group should advocate for rigid natural guidelines, support reasonable practices, and oppose overreliance on businesses that present huge ecological dangers. Thusly, they safeguard their biological systems as well as strengthen their economies against the possible aftermath of ecological fiascos.

In pondering these verifiable occasions and the examples they offer, it becomes obvious that versatility is a continuous cycle — a powerful transaction between prescience, flexibility, and shared strength. Waterfront economies, confronting a variety of difficulties in a consistently developing world, have the potential chance to mesh these examples into the texture of their networks, guaranteeing that the versatility constructed today prepares for a more manageable and prosperous tomorrow.

As the tides of progress keep on molding the waterfront scene, the accounts of Galveston, the Residue Bowl travelers, the Baltic Expresses, the Indian Sea wave survivors, and the Deepwater Skyline repercussions act as reference points of motivation. They advise us that flexibility isn't simply a reaction to difficulty however a purposeful, aggregate work to construct a future that can endure the tempests — whether they be normal, monetary, or international — that lie not too far off.

In the consistently changing scene of the worldwide economy, organizations are ceaselessly stood up to with challenges going from monetary slumps and market vulnerabilities to mechanical disturbances and unexpected worldwide occasions. Flourishing in violent monetary circumstances requires a vital and versatile methodology that goes past simple endurance. It requests versatility, development, and a promise to ceaseless improvement. This exhaustive investigation dives into methodologies organizations can utilize to endure the hardships as well as to flourish in the midst of disturbance.

Nimble Plans of action:

The foundation of flourishing in violent financial circumstances is the reception of coordinated plans of action. Nimbleness permits organizations to quickly answer changing business sector elements, client inclinations, and outside challenges. Instead of sticking to inflexible designs, coordinated organizations focus on adaptability, empowering them to turn rapidly, investigate new open doors, and adjust their methodologies to line up with the advancing monetary scene.

Key Development:

Embracing development as an essential basic positions organizations to flourish in the midst of financial vulnerabilities. This includes creating inventive items and administrations as well as encouraging a culture of ceaseless improvement and innovativeness inside the association. Organizations that focus on advancement are better prepared to remain in front of the opposition, meet developing client needs, and recognize novel income streams.

Client Driven Concentration:

A client driven approach is critical for business progress in fierce financial circumstances. Understanding and answering client needs, inclinations, and input encourages reliability and flexibility. By setting the client at the focal point of dynamic cycles, organizations can fit their contributions to fulfill market needs, guaranteeing supported significance and a steadfast client base in any event, during monetary slumps.

Computerized Change:

Computerized change is at this point not an extravagance yet a need for organizations looking to flourish in the present monetary scene. Embracing computerized advancements upgrades functional effectiveness, further develops client encounters, and gives important information to informed direction. Organizations that embrace advanced change are better situated to explore vulnerabilities, influence arising valuable open doors, and remain serious in an undeniably computerized world.

Vital Expense The executives:

Reasonable expense the board is fundamental for business flexibility. During tempestuous financial circumstances, organizations ought to lead intensive audits of their functional costs, distinguishing regions for improvement without compromising center functionalities. Vital expense the board includes focusing on speculations that line up with business needs, expanding functional proficiency, and executing lean practices to improve generally monetary wellbeing.

Monetary Flexibility and Possibility Arranging:

Building monetary flexibility includes laying out a strong monetary establishment equipped for enduring financial shocks. This incorporates keeping up with sound income, overseeing obligation mindfully, and having possibility assets to address unexpected difficulties. Organizations ought to lead situation investigations to expect possible monetary slumps, empowering them to foster proactive alternate courses of action that defend their monetary soundness.

Key Organizations and Coordinated efforts:

Cooperative associations with different organizations, industry players, or even contenders can improve versatility and encourage advancement. Key joint efforts empower organizations to pool assets, share ability, and aggregately address difficulties. By building an organization of believed accomplices, organizations make a cooperative environment that reinforces their capacity to explore financial vulnerabilities and gain by shared open doors.

Representative Strengthening and Reskilling:

Representatives are a business' most noteworthy resource, and their strengthening is basic to flexibility. Organizations ought to put resources into representative turn of events, giving open doors to upskilling and reskilling to line up with changing position necessities. An enabled and versatile labor force is better prepared to add to the association's flexibility, drive development, and explore advancing monetary circumstances.

Worldwide Market Enhancement:

Depending on a solitary market makes organizations powerless against monetary vacillations in that particular locale. To upgrade versatility, organizations ought to consider differentiating their market presence internationally. Venturing into new business sectors gives a cushion against limited monetary slumps and opens roads for development in districts with additional great financial circumstances.

Key Showcasing and Marking:

Key showcasing is significant for keeping up with perceivability and pertinence in fierce financial circumstances. Organizations ought to make versatile showcasing procedures that stress their novel incentives, connect with clients really, and separate them from contenders. Steady marking fabricates trust and client faithfulness, giving a strong groundwork to organizations to flourish even in testing financial environments.

Internet business and Online Presence:

The computerized period has changed customer ways of behaving, making a web-based presence fundamental for business achievement. Embracing web based business and laying out a vigorous internet based presence empowers organizations to contact a more extensive crowd, differentiate income streams, and adjust to changing buyer inclinations. A viable computerized system adds to business versatility by giving roads to proceeded with development even in testing monetary circumstances.

Risk The executives and Situation Arranging:

Proactive gamble the executives includes distinguishing, surveying, and relieving potential dangers that could affect business tasks. Situation arranging empowers organizations to expect different financial situations and foster methodologies to address what is going on. By adopting a comprehensive strategy to gamble with the executives, organizations improve their capacity to answer really to unexpected difficulties and limit the effect of monetary choppiness.

Manageable Strategic policies:

Manageability is as of now not simply a popular expression; it is a critical driver of business flexibility. Feasible practices add to natural and social obligation as well as line up with advancing shopper inclinations. Organizations that coordinate maintainability into their tasks frequently appreciate cost reserve funds, upgraded brand notoriety, and expanded flexibility despite changing business sector assumptions.

Client Maintenance Techniques:

While obtaining new clients is fundamental, holding existing clients is similarly basic for business strength. Executing client maintenance procedures, for example, faithfulness programs, customized encounters, and superb client support, reinforces the client business relationship. Faithful clients are bound to stay with a business during financial slumps, giving a steady income base.

Versatile Authority:

Authority assumes a vital part in directing organizations through tempestuous financial circumstances. Versatile initiative includes an eagerness to embrace change, pursue informed choices, and motivate the association to explore vulnerabilities. Pioneers who cultivate a culture of strength, spryness, and development contribute essentially to the general achievement and life span of the business.

Vital Consolidations and Acquisitions:

Consolidations and acquisitions can be key moves to improve business versatility. By obtaining reciprocal organizations or converging with key accomplices, organizations can get to new business sectors, advances, and ability pools. Painstakingly executed consolidations and acquisitions add to business development, broadening, and expanded seriousness, which are all fundamental for flourishing in fierce financial circumstances.

Virtual Entertainment Tuning in and Notoriety The board:

Virtual entertainment has turned into a useful asset for molding public discernment. Organizations ought to effectively pay attention to online discussions, screen client criticism, and answer speedily to arising issues. A hearty standing administration methodology includes constructing and keeping a positive brand picture, which is vital for strength during financial vulnerabilities.

Imaginative Evaluating Methodologies:

During monetary slumps, imaginative evaluating methodologies can give an upper hand. Organizations ought to investigate dynamic evaluating models, membership administrations, and worth added groups to take special care of changing purchaser ways of behaving. Adaptable valuing techniques draw in clients as well as add to income versatility notwithstanding monetary difficulties.

Lean and Proficient Tasks:

Working with proficiency and limiting waste is essential to business flexibility. Embracing lean practices guarantees that assets are used ideally, functional cycles are smoothed out, and costs are held under tight restraints. Organizations that focus on lean and effective tasks are better prepared to climate financial slumps while keeping an upper hand.

Information Driven Direction:

In a time of huge information, organizations that influence information for dynamic increase a critical benefit. Information driven bits of knowledge empower organizations to make educated, vital choices, recognize drifts, and anticipate market shifts. By integrating information examination into their dynamic cycles, organizations improve their capacity to answer proactively to monetary circumstances and client inclinations.

Emergency Correspondence and Straightforwardness:

Straightforward correspondence is essential during seasons of monetary vulnerability. Organizations ought to foster vigorous emergency correspondence designs that underscore straightforwardness, trustworthiness, and ideal updates. Keeping up with open correspondence with partners, including clients, workers, and accomplices, fabricates trust and certainty, adding to the general versatility of the business.

Government and Administrative Commitment:

Drawing in with government bodies and keeping up to date with administrative changes is fundamental for business versatility. Proactive cooperation in industry affiliations, support gatherings, and strategy conversations permits organizations to impact administrative choices and remain informed about potential changes that might affect their tasks. Administrative commitment adds to flexibility by guaranteeing organizations are good to go for consistence necessities.

Consistent Learning and Transformation:

Flexibility is a continuous interaction that requires a pledge to ceaseless learning and transformation. Organizations ought to develop a culture of interest, urge workers to remain refreshed on industry drifts, and be available to trying different things with groundbreaking thoughts. A promise to nonstop learning positions organizations to proactively change their procedures in light of developing monetary circumstances.

Interest in Innovative work:

Putting resources into innovative work (Research and development) is vital for long haul business flexibility. Research and development drives empower organizations to remain in front of industry patterns, enhance items and administrations, and stay serious in unique business sectors. Organizations that focus on Research and development are better situated to present state of the art arrangements and adjust to changing client requests.

Mental Versatility and Prosperity:

Past key and functional measures, organizations ought to likewise focus on the mental strength and prosperity of their labor force. Worker confidence, emotional wellness, and a positive working environment culture add to generally speaking hierarchical strength. Organizations that put resources into making a strong and even workplace are bound to have an inspired and versatile labor force.

Interest in Green and Feasible Practices:

Coordinating green and manageable practices into business activities isn't just morally capable yet additionally adds to flexibility. Buyers are progressively focusing on ecologically cognizant organizations, and manageable practices can prompt expense investment funds, improved brand notoriety, and long haul practicality. Organizations that line up with natural and social obligation patterns position themselves for flexibility in a changing business sector scene.

Production network Streamlining:

The versatility of a business is frequently interlaced with the strength of its store network. Organizations ought to survey their store network, recognize possible weaknesses, and execute methodologies to enhance and strengthen it. This incorporates enhancing providers, consolidating innovation for constant perceivability, and laying out alternate courses of action to successfully address interruptions.

Interest in Worker Preparing and Advancement:

Workers are a business' most significant resource, and putting resources into their preparation and improvement upgrades by and large versatility. Ceaseless learning programs, administration advancement drives, and cross-practical preparation engage representatives to adjust to developing jobs and obligations. A gifted and versatile labor force is better prepared to add to the business' flexibility during tempestuous times.

Develop a Culture of Advancement:

Developing a culture of advancement energizes workers at all levels to contribute thoughts, explore different avenues regarding new methodologies, and search out open doors for development. Organizations that cultivate an inventive culture are bound to adjust to changing financial circumstances, remain in front of contenders, and distinguish new roads for development.

Worldwide Financial Patterns Mindfulness:

Organizations working in a globalized economy should remain informed about worldwide monetary patterns. Changes in worldwide business sectors, exchange approaches, and international movements can have flowing impacts on neighborhood organizations. Attention to these patterns empowers organizations to proactively change their procedures and expect potential difficulties emerging from shifts in the more extensive financial scene.

Chapter 9

Charting the Future

In the steadily developing scene of human advancement, the demonstration of outlining what's to come is both a need and an honor. It includes a fragile dance between the known and the obscure, the past and the present, and the goals that fuel the human soul. This complex route isn't exclusively the space of visionaries or pioneers yet is an aggregate undertaking that connects with social orders, establishments, and people the same.

At its center, outlining what's to come is tied in with laying out steps to arrive at progress, figuring out the flows of progress, and saddling the breezes of development. It requires a mix of foreknowledge and versatility, a readiness to embrace vulnerability, and a guarantee to persistent learning. As we set out on this investigation of what lies ahead, we dive into the multi-layered elements of diagramming the future, investigating the difficulties, open doors, and moral contemplations that shape the direction of our aggregate process.

The mechanical scene remains as a conspicuous material whereupon what's in store is painted. Progressions in man-made brainpower, quantum processing, biotechnology, and other state of the art fields rethink the limits of human capacity as well as suggest significant conversation starters about the moral ramifications and cultural effect of these forward leaps. The persistent walk of innovation requests a smart way to deal with its incorporation into our lives, requiring a fragile harmony among development and moral obligation.

Man-made consciousness, for example, holds massive commitment in reforming enterprises, robotizing dreary assignments, and enlarging human navigation. However, the moral elements of simulated intelligence, including issues of inclination, responsibility, and the potential for work removal, highlight the requirement for a complete system that guides its turn of events and sending. Graphing the future, in this unique circumstance, requires a sharp consciousness of the moral tightrope that goes with mechanical advancement and a pledge to planning frameworks that line up with our qualities.

The extraordinary capability of innovation stretches out past the domain of computer based intelligence, incorporating the huge conceivable outcomes presented by quantum figuring. As we stand on the cusp of a quantum insurgency, the ramifications for cryptography, materials science, and enhancement calculations are significant. Outlining a future that consolidates quantum figuring requires specialized ability as well as a nuanced comprehension of the security, protection, and cultural ramifications that accompany quantum headways.

Biotechnology, one more boondocks of development, opens new vistas in medical care, farming, and then some. CRISPR quality altering innovation, for example, holds the commitment of killing hereditary illnesses, however it likewise prompts moral inquiries regarding the limits of hereditary control and the potential for unseen side-effects. In diagramming the eventual fate of biotechnology, a cautious assessment of the moral, legitimate, and social aspects is basic to guarantee that progress lines up with human qualities and regards the sacredness of life.

The mechanical embroidered artwork is interlaced with the strings of network and information. The ascent of the Web of Things (IoT) and the multiplication of interconnected gadgets rethink the texture of our regular routines. From brilliant homes to shrewd urban communities, the snare of network sets out uncommon open doors for effectiveness, accommodation, and advancement. Nonetheless, it additionally raises worries about information protection, security weaknesses, and the potential for misuse. Diagramming a future where network encourages progress while defending individual privileges requires a watchful and cooperative work to lay out powerful systems for information administration and online protection.

In the mission for mechanical headway, the moral contemplations reach out past the domain of science and designing. The plans of action that support the innovation business, with their accentuation on information adaptation and algorithmic navigation, shape the cultural scene.

Diagramming a future that bridles the advantages of innovation while moderating its negative externalities requests a reconsideration of strategic policies, corporate obligation, and the power elements that arise in the computerized age.

As we explore the intricacies of the innovative wilderness, the cultural effects of progress come into sharp concentration. The elements of work and business go through significant changes directly following mechanization and man-made intelligence. Outlining a future that guarantees financial inclusivity requires a change in perspective in training, labor force improvement, and social strategies. Embracing the capability of innovation to expand human capacities as opposed to supplant them is a vital principle of this forward-looking methodology, cultivating a future where development and value remain forever inseparable.

Couple with mechanical headways, the ecological difficulties that loom not too far off request critical consideration in our diagramming representing things to come. Environmental change, asset consumption, and biodiversity misfortune address basic dangers that require an aggregate and deliberate exertion. The change to manageable practices, sustainable power sources, and round economies becomes foremost chasing a future that offsets human advancement with environmental stewardship.

Graphing the future notwithstanding natural difficulties requires a takeoff from conventional models of utilization and creation. It includes reconsidering our relationship with the planet, taking on regenerative practices, and encouraging a feeling of obligation for the prosperity of people in the future. The crossing points of innovation and manageability become pivotal fields where development and ecological cognizance unite to shape a future that isn't just prosperous yet additionally strong.

In the domain of medical services, what's in store unfurls with the commitment of customized medication, genomic treatments, and headways in preventive consideration. The union of information examination, genomics, and clinical advances opens new outskirts in sickness recognition, therapy, and medical services conveyance. Be that as it may, moral contemplations with respect to protection, assent, and fair admittance to medical care administrations pose a potential threat in this scene. Outlining the eventual fate of medical care requests a comprehensive methodology that consolidates logical development with moral systems to guarantee that the advantages of clinical advancement are open to all.

Schooling, as the foundation of cultural advancement, goes through a change during the time spent outlining what's to come. The conventional models of instruction, with their accentuation on repetition retention and state sanctioned testing, give way to additional dynamic and versatile methodologies. The joining of innovation, customized opportunities for growth, and an emphasis on decisive reasoning furnishes people with the abilities expected to explore a consistently evolving scene.

The democratization of training, worked with by online stages and open-access assets, turns into a main impetus in cultivating a future where information is open to all, rising above geographic and financial boundaries.

In the great embroidery of human development, the strings of culture, workmanship, and articulation weave a story that rises above the utilitarian parts of progress. Outlining what's to come includes protecting and sustaining the social legacy that characterizes social orders, encouraging innovativeness, and embracing the variety of human articulation. The advanced age, with its phenomenal admittance to data and worldwide network, gives the two valuable open doors and difficulties in such manner. The conservation of social personalities and the advancement of comprehensive stories become basic parts of graphing a future that esteems the wealth of human legacy.

Chasing progress, the job of administration arises as a basic calculate forming the shapes representing things to come. The customary models of administration, with their progressive designs and slow dynamic cycles, face moves in adjusting to the quick speed of mechanical and cultural change. Graphing a future that is responsive, comprehensive, and responsible requires a rethinking of administration models, integrating standards of straightforwardness, resident investment, and moral oversight.

The worldwide scene, set apart by interconnectedness and association, presents the two open doors for coordinated effort and difficulties of international intricacy. Outlining the future with regards to worldwide relations requests a nuanced comprehension of international elements, a pledge to discretionary exchange, and an acknowledgment of the common obligation regarding worldwide difficulties. Issues, for example, environmental change, general wellbeing emergencies, and financial incongruities highlight the requirement for agreeable systems that rise above public limits.

Chasing diagramming the future, the job of people as influencers comes to the very front. Our decisions as customers, the qualities we maintain, and the manner in which we draw in with innovation and society by and large shape the direction of progress. The strengthening of people through schooling, admittance to data, and the development of decisive reasoning turns into a key part in diagramming a future that isn't just mechanically progressed yet in addition socially.

Morals, as a core value in the outlining representing things to come, penetrates each feature of human undertaking. It includes a promise to standards of equity, value, and regard for common liberties. In the domain of innovation, moral contemplations reach out past the advancement of calculations and man-made intelligence to envelop issues of computerized privileges, online protection, and the effect of innovation on weak populaces. Outlining a future that maintains moral guide lines requires an aggregate work to lay out standards, guidelines, and responsibility components that defend the prosperity of people and networks.

The speed increase of progress, driven by mechanical advancement, cultural development, and natural difficulties, urges us to embrace a mentality of consistent transformation. Outlining what's to come turns into an iterative interaction, requiring an eagerness to reevaluate suppositions, gain from disappointments, and embrace the illustrations of the present. The flexibility of people, networks, and establishments turns into a pivotal calculate exploring the vulnerabilities that portray the excursion forward.

In the fabulous embroidery of outlining the future, the exchange of science, innovation, morals, and cultural elements makes a mind boggling and dynamic scene. It is a scene where the strings of progress are woven with the strands of human creativity, moral contemplations, and a promise to the prosperity of the planet and its occupants. As we set out on this excursion, the decisions, the qualities we maintain, and the cooperative endeavors we participate in become the compass that guides us toward a future that isn't just graphed however created with reason and care.

9.1 Exploration of emerging trends in coastal commerce

The huge spans of shores have filled in as basic conductors for trade all through mankind's set of experiences. From the clamoring ports of old civilizations to the present day uber ports working with worldwide exchange, beach front locales assume a critical part in forming monetary scenes. In the contemporary setting, the investigation of arising patterns in waterfront business becomes fundamental as mechanical, ecological, and international variables merge to rethink the elements of oceanic exchange.

One of the noticeable patterns reshaping beach front trade is the approach of brilliant ports and sea planned operations. The reconciliation of trend setting innovations like Web of Things (IoT), man-made consciousness (simulated intelligence), and blockchain into port activities improves proficiency, straightforwardness, and security. Savvy ports influence sensor organizations to screen and streamline different parts of port exercises, from compartment following to prescient upkeep of framework. These innovative mediations smooth out activities as well as add to lessening ecological effects by limiting fuel utilization and discharges.

The ascent of independent delivery addresses one more extraordinary pattern in waterfront business. Automated vessels, controlled by computer based intelligence and navigational frameworks, are ready to alter sea transport. These independent boats offer the potential for expanded effectiveness, decreased functional expenses, and further developed wellbeing. Be that as it may, the far reaching reception of independent delivery delivers difficulties connected with administrative structures, network protection, and the likely dislodging of oceanic positions. As waterfront business embraces independence, a fragile equilibrium should be struck among development and the moral, lawful, and cultural contemplations related with automated oceanic frameworks.

Natural manageability is a point of convergence in the investigation of arising patterns in seaside trade. Environmental change and natural debasement present existential dangers, provoking the oceanic business to embrace eco-accommodating practices. The improvement of green ports, using sustainable power sources, energized hardware, and eco-accommodating framework, lines up with worldwide endeavors to diminish the carbon impression of oceanic exercises. Furthermore, the change to cleaner drive innovations, like electric and half and half impetus for ships, mirrors a promise to maintainable waterfront business.

The Cold district arises as a boondocks in waterfront trade because of the dissolving of ocean ice, opening new sea courses and potential open doors. The Northern Ocean Course, crossing the Cold waters, abbreviates the distance among Europe and Asia, offering possible expense investment funds for delivery organizations. Notwithstanding, the expanded oceanic action in the Icy raises worries about ecological effects, environment disturbance, and the requirement for powerful security measures. The investigation of arising patterns in beach front business reaches out to the Cold, requiring a harmony between monetary open doors and ecological stewardship in this delicate biological system.

Digitalization is a main impetus behind the change of seaside trade. The computerized upset, set apart by the multiplication of information examination, distributed computing, and availability, empowers continuous checking, information driven navigation, and upgraded correspondence in oceanic tasks. From robotized freight following to electronic route frameworks, digitalization streamlines the progression of data across the sea store network, cultivating productivity and versatility in waterfront business.

Exchange help and worldwide cooperation assume a urgent part in molding the eventual fate of waterfront business. The rise of provincial and worldwide economic deals, combined with cooperative drives for framework improvement, upgrades network and advances monetary development in seaside locales. Endeavors to smooth out customs techniques, diminish exchange hindrances, and cultivate cross-line collaboration add to the dynamic quality of seaside business. As countries try to enhance and reinforce their exchange organizations, the investigation of arising patterns includes an essential spotlight on worldwide organizations and exchange partnerships.

With regards to seaside trade, the blue economy arises as an all encompassing and economical way to deal with marine-related exercises. Past customary transportation and port activities, the blue economy includes areas like fisheries, hydroponics, the travel industry, and environmentally friendly power. The dependable and comprehensive improvement of the blue economy includes offsetting monetary objectives with natural preservation and local area prosperity. As waterfront districts saddle the capability of the blue economy, cautious preparation and adherence to economical practices become basic for long haul practicality.

Security contemplations pose a potential threat in the investigation of arising patterns in waterfront trade. Oceanic courses are helpless against a scope of dangers, including theft, psychological oppression, and sneaking. The sending of cutting edge innovations, like satellite reconnaissance, automated airborne vehicles, and incorporated security frameworks, improves the wellbeing and security of waterfront waters. Cooperative endeavors between countries to battle sea dangers, combined with worldwide oceanic security arrangements, add to establishing a solid climate for beach front trade to flourish.

The development of online business and the rising interest for quicker, more solid delivery administrations have significant ramifications for waterfront trade. The ascent of online retail has prompted a flood in containerized freight traffic, requiring productive and dexterous port tasks. Beach front districts are seeing the development and modernization of planned operations centers to oblige the changing idea of shopper conduct and worldwide exchange designs. The joining of innovation, mechanization, and information examination into the coordinated factors and store network biological system becomes fundamental in fulfilling the developing needs of online business in waterfront trade.

As the world wrestles with the effects of the Coronavirus pandemic, the versatility of beach front business comes to the bleeding edge. The pandemic has upset worldwide inventory chains, influencing oceanic exchange and port tasks. The investigation of arising patterns in waterfront trade includes adjusting to the difficulties presented by pandemics and other worldwide emergencies. From digitalizing documentation cycles to executing wellbeing and security conventions, seaside districts are rethinking their readiness and reaction components to guarantee the congruity of oceanic exercises despite unexpected interruptions.

International elements shape the scene of seaside business, affecting shipping lanes, port turn of events, and global oceanic arrangements. The essential meaning of specific oceanic chokepoints, like the Waterway of Hormuz and the South China Ocean, highlights the international contemplations innate in waterfront business. The investigation of arising patterns in this setting includes a nuanced comprehension of international movements, discretionary relations, and the international ramifications of foundation undertakings like ports and sea halls.

The consolidation of man-made reasoning (artificial intelligence) and enormous information examination into sea tasks is an extraordinary pattern that upgrades effectiveness, security, and dynamic in waterfront trade. Simulated intelligence calculations dissect huge datasets to improve course arranging, foresee support needs, and upgrade by and large vessel execution. Huge information investigation empower continuous checking of oceanic exercises, taking into account proactive direction and hazard the board. As beach front locales embrace these mechanical headways, the mix of artificial intelligence and large information turns into a foundation in the development of savvy and strong seaside trade.

All in all, the investigation of arising patterns in seaside trade unfurls as a multi-layered venture enveloping mechanical development, natural supportability, international contemplations, and cultural elements. From the combination of brilliant advancements and independence in oceanic activities to the basic of ecological stewardship and the difficulties presented by international movements, seaside trade remains at the junction of change. Exploring this perplexing scene requires a vital and cooperative methodology, including partners from states, businesses, and networks. As beach front areas graph the course for the eventual fate of oceanic exchange, the amalgamation of advancement, supportability, and flexibility turns into the compass directing the development of seaside business in the 21st hundred years.

9.2 Interviews with futurists and industry experts on the future of maritime trade

In the journey to unwind the fate of oceanic exchange, drawing in with futurists and industry specialists gives important bits of knowledge into the patterns, difficulties, and open doors that lie ahead. These visionary people offer points of view formed by their profound comprehension of innovative progressions, international movements, and ecological contemplations. Through interviews with futurists and industry specialists, a nuanced investigation representing things to come of oceanic exchange arises, enveloping the effect of development, the development of shipping lanes, and the basic of maintainability.

One key topic that rises up out of these conversations is the extraordinary job of innovation in molding the fate of oceanic exchange. Dr. Maria Hernandez, a futurist spend significant time in transportation and operations, underlines the urgent job of digitalization in reforming the oceanic business. She notes, "We are seeing a change in perspective in how oceanic exchange works. The joining of advances like man-made consciousness, blockchain, and the Web of Things is essentially adjusting how boats are made due, freight is followed, and ports are worked."

Hernandez highlights the meaning of brilliant ports as a key part in the mechanical development of sea exchange. "Brilliant ports influence state of the art innovations to upgrade effectiveness, decrease functional expenses, and limit ecological effect," she makes sense of. "The utilization of sensors, robotization, and information examination enhances different parts of port activities, from freight taking care of to support booking. This smoothes out processes as well as adds to a more practical and versatile sea framework."

In an equal vein, Chief James Anderson, a carefully prepared oceanic industry master with many years of involvement with ocean, reveals insight into the effect of independence on sea exchange. "Independent delivery is presently not a modern idea; it's turning into a reality," Anderson states. "Automated vessels, directed by cutting edge navigational frameworks and man-made reasoning, can possibly reshape the whole scene of oceanic vehicle. While there are difficulties to survive, including administrative systems and network protection concerns, the advantages regarding proficiency, security, and cost-adequacy are critical."

The idea of independent transportation brings up moral contemplations and issues about the fate of oceanic work. Commander Anderson recognizes these worries, expressing, "The human component in sea tasks stays critical. While we embrace independence for its benefits, we should guarantee a decent methodology that jelly oceanic positions, focuses on security, and addresses the moral elements of automated frameworks."

Natural manageability arises as a focal topic in conversations about the eventual fate of oceanic exchange. Dr. Emily Chen, a natural futurist work in the crossing point of biology and business, features the basic of taking on eco-accommodating practices in seaside locales. "The sea business plays a basic part to play in moderating environmental change and decreasing its ecological impression," says Chen. "The improvement of green ports, the progress to cleaner impetus advances, and the execution of reasonable practices in fisheries and hydroponics are fundamental parts of a future where sea exchange coincides amicably with the climate."

Dr. Chen stresses the significance of worldwide coordinated effort in tending to ecological difficulties. "Environmental change is a common worldwide concern, and beach front districts should cooperate to take on and carry out economical practices. This includes mechanical developments as well as strategy structures that advance natural stewardship and the capable utilization of marine assets."

The Icy district, frequently alluded to as the "new outskirts" in sea exchange, flashes extreme interest among futurists and industry specialists the same. Dr. Nikolai Petrov, an international examiner having some expertise in Icy issues, shares his experiences on the developing elements in the locale. "The softening of Cold ocean ice is opening up new sea courses, introducing the two valuable open doors and difficulties," Petrov makes sense of. "The Northern Ocean Course, which associates Europe and Asia through the Cold, can possibly altogether abbreviate delivering distances and lessen travel times. In any case, the expanded human action in the Cold additionally raises worries about natural effect, native freedoms, and international strains."

Petrov stresses the requirement for a cooperative and reasonable way to deal with Icy oceanic exchange. "The Icy is a fragile biological system, and any disturbance could have sweeping results. Worldwide collaboration, adherence to natural guidelines, and regard for the freedoms of native networks are non-debatable components in diagramming the fate of oceanic exchange the Cold."

The computerized upheaval's effect on sea exchange is a repetitive topic in conversations with industry specialists. Dr. Sophia Lee, an innovation futurist work in computerized change, dives into the meaning of digitalization in reshaping the sea production network. "Digitalization isn't just about integrating innovation into existing cycles; it's an essential change in how the whole production network works," Lee states.

"From computerized documentation and constant following to prescient investigation and shrewd planned operations, digitalization upgrades the proficiency and versatility of oceanic exchange."

Lee recognizes that the inescapable reception of computerized innovations requires a social shift inside the business. "Embracing digitalization isn't just about innovation; it's tied in with cultivating an outlook of development, coordinated effort, and flexibility. Partners across the sea store network, from transporters to port administrators, need to put resources into advanced education and make a biological system that supports trial and error and nonstop improvement."

Exchange help and worldwide cooperation arise as basic variables in molding the eventual fate of sea exchange. Dr. Carlos Rodriguez, a specialist in worldwide exchange and monetary turn of events, underlines the interconnected idea of worldwide exchange organizations. "Beach front districts are essential hubs in the worldwide exchange organization, and the fate of sea exchange depends on powerful exchange assistance components," Rodriguez notes. "The rise of territorial economic deals, the decrease of exchange obstructions, and the advancement of strong foundation add to the liveliness of waterfront trade."

Rodriguez features the job of exchange unions molding the future scene. "In a period set apart by financial reliance, exchange coalitions become key resources.

Cooperative endeavors between countries, whether through existing exchange coalitions or two-sided arrangements, improve the intensity of waterfront districts and establish a helpful climate for oceanic exchange to prosper."

The blue economy, including different marine-related areas, arises as an all encompassing way to deal with seaside business. Dr. Olivia Turner, a sea life scientist and futurist, stresses the capability of the blue economy to offset monetary improvement with ecological preservation. "The seas are not only a wellspring of trade; they are crucial biological systems that help life on The planet," Turner states. "The dependable advancement of areas like fisheries, hydroponics, the travel industry, and environmentally friendly power is vital for guaranteeing the drawn out manageability of waterfront locales."

Turner highlights the significance of partner joint effort in the blue economy. "Offsetting monetary objectives with ecological preservation requires a multidisciplinary approach. Coordinated effort between researchers, policymakers, industry partners, and neighborhood networks is fundamental to guarantee that the blue economy turns into a power for positive change as opposed to a danger to marine biological systems."

Security contemplations in oceanic exchange possess a noticeable spot in interviews with industry specialists. Back Naval commander Sarah Mill operator, a sea security master with a recognized profession in maritime tasks, gives experiences into the developing idea of sea dangers.

"Oceanic courses are helpless to a scope of safety challenges, including robbery, illegal intimidation, and unlawful exercises," Mill operator notices. "The sending of cutting edge innovations, like satellite reconnaissance, automated aeronautical vehicles, and incorporated security frameworks, improves the wellbeing and security of waterfront waters."

Mill operator stresses the requirement for worldwide participation to address sea security challenges. "Sea security is a worldwide worry that requires cooperative endeavors. Global sea security arrangements, joint watches, and data sharing components are instrumental in establishing a protected climate for sea exchange to flourish."

The ascent of web based business and its effect on oceanic exchange surfaces as a huge pattern conversations with industry specialists. Dr. Jonathan Dough puncher, a financial analyst spend significant time in exchange and business, clarifies the ramifications of the web based business blast on delivery and operations. "The shift toward online retail has changed shopper conduct, prompting an extraordinary interest for effective and dependable delivery administrations," Pastry specialist notes. "Beach front districts are seeing the development and modernization of coordinated operations centers to meet the advancing necessities of internet business, and this pattern is reshaping the elements of oceanic exchange."

Dough puncher accentuates the job of innovation in adjusting to the requests of online business. "From last-mile conveyance answers for stockroom computerization, innovation assumes a vital part in guaranteeing the nimbleness and responsiveness of sea exchange to the necessities of web based business. Developments in coordinated operations and production network the executives become key drivers in store for seaside trade."

As the world fights with the effects of the Coronavirus pandemic, the strength of sea exchange comes to the front line conversations with industry specialists. Dr. Ahmed Khan, a general wellbeing master with an emphasis on sea wellbeing and security, gives experiences into the difficulties presented by pandemics and worldwide emergencies. "The pandemic has disturbed worldwide stock chains, influencing sea exchange and port tasks. The requirement for wellbeing and security measures, digitalization of documentation cycles, and possibility arranging has become more articulated," Khan states.

Khan stresses the significance of readiness even with unexpected disturbances. "Worldwide occasions, for example, pandemics and cataclysmic events require a reassessment of hazard the board and possibility arranging in sea exchange. The capacity to adjust rapidly to changing conditions and execute wellbeing conventions becomes essential to guaranteeing the coherence of sea exercises."

International contemplations and their effect on sea exchange are investigated in interviews with international examiners. Dr. Mei Ling, a specialist in oceanic international affairs, examines the essential meaning of specific sea chokepoints.

"The control of key sea chokepoints, like the Waterway of Hormuz and the South China Ocean, has international ramifications for worldwide shipping lanes," Ling makes sense of. "Understanding the international elements in these areas is critical for waterfront locales trying to explore the intricacies of global oceanic relations."

Ling highlights the requirement for strategy and participation in tending to international difficulties. "International strains can influence oceanic exchange, yet cooperative strategic endeavors can alleviate gambles. Taking part in discourse, regarding global standards, and maintaining the standards of opportunity of route add to a steady and secure climate for beach front trade."

Consolidating man-made brainpower (man-made intelligence) and huge information examination into sea tasks arises as a groundbreaking pattern in conversations with industry specialists. Commander Mei Lin, a sea innovation trained professional, examines the effect of man-made intelligence on vessel execution. "Simulated intelligence calculations investigate immense datasets to streamline course arranging, foresee upkeep needs, and improve generally vessel execution. Huge information examination empower constant checking of oceanic exercises, considering proactive navigation and hazard the executives," Lin makes sense of.

Lin stresses the requirement for extensive coordinated effort in outfitting the capability of simulated intelligence and huge information. "The mix of simulated intelligence and huge information isn't an independent exertion by individual partners. It requires coordinated effort across the oceanic inventory network, from delivery organizations and port administrators to innovation suppliers. By encouraging a biological system of shared information and bits of knowledge, the business can all in all drive the advancement of brilliant and versatile waterfront trade."

All in all, the meetings with futurists and industry specialists reveal a rich embroidery of bits of knowledge into the eventual fate of oceanic exchange. The combination of mechanical development, ecological supportability, international elements, and cultural contemplations shapes a scene that is both intricate and dynamic. From the joining of savvy advances and the ascent of independent delivery to the basic of maintainability and the difficulties presented by worldwide occasions, waterfront business remains at the junction of change. Exploring this complicated territory requires a cooperative, versatile, and ground breaking come nearer from partners across the oceanic business. The union of advancement, manageability, and strength arises as the core values in outlining the course for the eventual fate of oceanic exchange the 21st hundred years.

9.3 Recommendations for businesses to prepare for and capitalize on future opportunities in coastal commerce

As the sea business goes through quick change driven by mechanical headways, ecological contemplations, and moving worldwide elements, organizations participated in waterfront trade face the two difficulties and potential open doors. Exploring this mind boggling scene requires key foreknowledge, flexibility, and a proactive way to deal with influence arising patterns. This article gives extensive proposals to organizations to plan for and gain by future open doors in seaside trade.

Embrace Digitalization and Brilliant Advancements:

The combination of computerized advances and savvy arrangements is vital for organizations working in seaside trade. Embrace digitalization across the whole inventory network, from port tasks to transportation coordinated operations. Carry out cutting edge innovations like the Web of Things (IoT), computerized reasoning (artificial intelligence), and blockchain to advance cycles, upgrade proficiency, and work on by and large execution. Brilliant ports, furnished with sensor organizations and robotized frameworks, assume a crucial part in smoothing out tasks and decreasing expenses. Organizations ought to put resources into the vital framework and develop a computerized culture to remain cutthroat in the developing oceanic scene.

Put resources into Independent Delivery and Route:

Independent delivery addresses the fate of oceanic exchange. Organizations ought to investigate interests in independent vessels, consolidating computer based intelligence driven route frameworks and automated advances. While this shift might require significant beginning speculations, the drawn out benefits with regards to functional proficiency, wellbeing, and cost-viability are critical. Team up with innovation suppliers and administrative bodies to guarantee a smooth change to independent transportation, tending to administrative systems, network safety concerns, and moral contemplations.

Focus on Natural Supportability:

Natural cognizance is at this point not a choice yet a need for organizations in beach front business. Embrace reasonable practices, put resources into eco-accommodating advances, and change to cleaner impetus frameworks. Create and stick to green port drives, consolidating environmentally friendly power sources, charged hardware, and reasonable foundation. Participate in dependable fisheries and hydroponics works on, adding to the safeguarding of marine biological systems. Organizations that focus on ecological manageability meet administrative necessities as well as appeal to shoppers and financial backers progressively worried about corporate obligation.

Investigate Open doors in the Cold:

With the dissolving of Cold ocean ice opening new sea courses, organizations ought to evaluate open doors in Icy exchange. The Northern Ocean Course presents a more limited way among Europe and Asia, offering possible expense investment funds. Assess the possibility of using these courses for transportation and investigate organizations with Cold countries for framework improvement. Be that as it may, organizations should move toward Cold business with a promise to natural security, native privileges, and feasible practices to guarantee capable commitment to this biologically delicate district.

Embrace Internet business Operations:

The ascent of online business is reshaping customer conduct and, subsequently, strategies requests. Organizations in beach front trade ought to adjust their activities to oblige the rising volume of containerized freight driven by online retail. Modernize and grow coordinated operations centers to meet the prerequisites of web based business, consolidating robotization, ongoing following, and proficient last-mile conveyance arrangements. Cooperation with web based business stages and operations suppliers is essential to remaining lithe and receptive to the advancing requirements of this unique market.

Put resources into Advanced Proficiency and Labor force Improvement:

As innovation becomes basic to seaside trade, organizations should put resources into advanced education and labor force improvement. Furnish workers with the abilities important to explore computerized devices, break down information, and influence arising advances. Preparing programs, organizations with instructive foundations, and ceaseless learning drives add to a labor force that isn't just versatile yet additionally equipped for driving development. A carefully proficient labor force is a resource in executing and boosting the advantages of digitalization and mechanical progressions.

Take part in Worldwide Exchange Collusions:

The worldwide idea of sea exchange requires dynamic cooperation global exchange collusions. Organizations ought to take part in local and worldwide economic accords that work with the progression of products and decrease exchange obstructions. Coordinated effort with global accomplices improves seriousness and opens up new business sectors. Remain informed about exchange approaches, levies, and international advancements that might influence global exchange. Utilizing the advantages of exchange coalitions positions organizations decisively in the worldwide oceanic biological system.

Differentiate into the Blue Economy:

The blue economy, enveloping areas like fisheries, hydroponics, the travel industry, and sustainable power, offers differentiated open doors for organizations in seaside business. Investigate interests in reasonable fisheries, capable hydroponics rehearses, and eco-accommodating the travel industry drives.

The improvement of seaward wind and marine energy projects adds to both monetary development and natural supportability. Enhancement into the blue economy extends income streams as well as adjusts organizations to the standards of capable and comprehensive sea advancement.

Improve Sea Safety efforts:

Security stays a basic worry in beach front trade. Organizations ought to put resources into cutting edge safety efforts, including satellite observation, automated elevated vehicles, and incorporated security frameworks. Team up with oceanic security organizations, take part in joint watches, and share data to relieve security gambles. Consistence with global oceanic security arrangements and adherence to best practices in network protection add to establishing a solid and stable climate for sea exchange tasks.

Encourage a Culture of Development and Flexibility:

In a quickly developing sea scene, cultivating a culture of development and versatility is critical to remaining ahead. Urge workers to contribute thoughts, explore different avenues regarding new innovations, and embrace an outlook of constant improvement. Lay out development center points or associations with innovation new businesses to remain at the front line of mechanical headways. Organizations that develop a culture of development are better situated to explore vulnerabilities and gain by arising open doors in the consistently changing seaside trade area.

Plan for Worldwide Emergencies and Pandemics:

Late worldwide occasions, including the Coronavirus pandemic, feature the significance of readiness for unexpected interruptions. Organizations ought to foster strong alternate courses of action, execute wellbeing and security conventions, and digitalize documentation cycles to upgrade strength. Team up with applicable specialists, industry affiliations, and wellbeing associations to remain informed about likely dangers and best practices in overseeing worldwide emergencies. A proactive and arranged approach guarantees the congruity of sea exercises during testing times.

Grasp International Elements:

International contemplations fundamentally impact sea exchange. Organizations ought to put resources into understanding the international elements of key sea chokepoints, shipping lanes, and vital locales. Remain informed about international movements, conciliatory relations, and possible effects on shipping lanes. Take part in discourse with applicable partners, including legislative bodies and international examiners, to explore the intricacies of global oceanic relations. Proactive commitment with international contemplations permits organizations to expect difficulties and pursue informed key choices.

Team up for Information Sharing and Interoperability:

In a period where information is a basic resource, organizations ought to effectively take part in drives for information sharing and interoperability. Team up with industry partners to lay out normal information guidelines, share pertinent data, and make interoperable frameworks. Shared information stages upgrade perceivability across the store network, work with smoother joint effort, and add to generally speaking industry effectiveness. Organizations that focus on information joint effort position themselves as necessary supporters of an associated and smoothed out seaside trade environment.

Integrate Round Economy Standards:

Economical and capable strategic approaches include taking on roundabout economy standards. Organizations ought to expect to limit squander, reuse materials, and add to the circularity of assets inside the sea store network. Execute reusing programs, investigate the utilization of economical bundling, and take on rehearses that lessen the ecological effect of tasks. Round economy standards line up with natural supportability objectives as well as add to long haul strength and dependable strategic policies.

Take part in Local area Effort and Social Obligation:

Waterfront trade organizations are naturally associated with neighborhood networks. Participate in local area outreach programs, add to nearby advancement drives, and focus on friendly obligation. Lay out associations with neighborhood associations, support schooling and preparing programs, and put resources into projects that upgrade the prosperity of encompassing networks. Organizations that effectively take part in friendly obligation drives construct positive connections, encourage altruism, and add to the by and large financial advancement of the districts they work in.

The sea business, a foundation of worldwide exchange and financial turn of events, is going through huge changes moved by mechanical headways, ecological objectives, and developing customer ways of behaving. Organizations participated in beach front trade should explore the ongoing intricacies as well as decisively position themselves to gain by future open doors. This far reaching guide presents noteworthy suggestions for organizations to flourish in the steadily developing scene of beach front trade.

Embrace Advanced Change:

The underpinning of future outcome in beach front trade lies in embracing computerized change. The combination of state of the art advancements, like the Web of Things (IoT), man-made consciousness (computer based intelligence), and blockchain, is fundamental. Organizations ought to put resources into powerful advanced framework to improve activities, upgrade proficiency, and encourage development. The progress to brilliant ports, furnished with sensor organizations and computerized frameworks, is an essential push toward a more lithe and responsive beach front trade biological system.

Investigate Independence in Delivery:

Independent delivery is arising as a groundbreaking pattern in oceanic exchange. Organizations ought to effectively investigate interests in independent vessels and route frameworks. The execution of artificial intelligence driven innovations can upset oceanic activities, offering advantages like expanded productivity, upgraded wellbeing, and cost-viability. While exploring administrative systems and online protection concerns is essential, organizations that pioneer independent arrangements position themselves as pioneers in store for beach front business.

Focus on Natural Manageability:

Natural cognizance is presently not a simple pattern yet a business basic. Waterfront trade organizations should focus on maintainability to line up with worldwide natural objectives and shopper assumptions. Put resources into eco-accommodating advancements, progress to cleaner drive frameworks, and effectively take part in green port drives. Mindful fisheries and hydroponics rehearses add to the protection of marine biological systems, guaranteeing a harmony between monetary exercises and natural preservation.

Take advantage of Chances in the Cold:

The dissolving of Cold ocean ice presents new open doors for sea exchange. Organizations ought to assess the practicality of using the Northern Ocean Course, which associates Europe and Asia through the Cold. Vital associations with Cold countries for framework improvement are critical to opening the capability of this locale. Nonetheless, mindful commitment is vital, requiring a promise to ecological insurance, regard for native freedoms, and adherence to economical practices.

Adjust to Online business Planned operations:

The ascent of online business is reshaping planned operations requests in waterfront trade. Organizations should adjust their activities to oblige the flood in containerized freight driven by online retail. Modernizing strategies centers with computerization, ongoing following, and productive last-mile conveyance arrangements is fundamental. Team up with web based business stages and coordinated factors suppliers to remain receptive to the developing necessities of this powerful market, guaranteeing a strategic advantage in the time of computerized trade.

Put resources into Computerized Education and Labor force Advancement:

As innovation becomes basic to beach front trade, it is basic to put resources into labor force improvement. Organizations ought to focus on computerized proficiency drives to outfit workers with the abilities important to explore advanced devices and influence arising innovations. Preparing projects and organizations with instructive establishments add to building a labor force that isn't just versatile yet additionally fit for driving development in the computerized period.

Take part in Global Exchange Collusions:

Given the worldwide idea of sea exchange, dynamic support in global exchange collusions is fundamental. Organizations ought to participate in provincial and worldwide economic deals that work with the progression of merchandise and diminish exchange obstructions. Coordinated effort with global accomplices improves intensity and opens up new business sectors. Remaining informed about exchange arrangements, duties, and international improvements positions organizations decisively in the interconnected worldwide sea biological system.

Expand into the Blue Economy:

The blue economy offers expanded open doors for organizations in beach front trade. Investigate interests in reasonable fisheries, dependable hydroponics rehearses, and eco-accommodating the travel industry drives. The improvement of seaward wind and marine energy projects adds to both monetary development and ecological manageability. Expansion into the blue economy extends income streams as well as adjusts organizations to the standards of capable and comprehensive oceanic turn of events.

Improve Sea Safety efforts:

Security stays a vital worry in waterfront business. Organizations ought to put resources into cutting edge safety efforts, including satellite observation, automated elevated vehicles, and coordinated security frameworks. Team up with oceanic security organizations, take part in joint watches, and share data to moderate security chances. Consistence with global oceanic security arrangements and online protection best practices adds to establishing a safe and stable climate for sea exchange tasks.

Encourage a Culture of Development:

A culture of development is irreplaceable for organizations expecting to flourish in the developing scene of seaside trade. Urge workers to contribute thoughts, try different things with new innovations, and embrace a mentality of constant improvement. Laying out development centers or associations with innovation new companies cultivates a climate that stays at the front line of mechanical progressions. Organizations that develop a culture of advancement are better situated to explore vulnerabilities and benefit from arising open doors.

Get ready for Worldwide Emergencies and Pandemics:

Late worldwide occasions, including the Coronavirus pandemic, highlight the significance of readiness for unanticipated interruptions. Organizations ought to foster powerful alternate courses of action, execute wellbeing and security conventions, and digitalize documentation cycles to upgrade strength. Cooperation with pertinent specialists, industry affiliations, and wellbeing associations is essential for remaining informed about expected dangers and best practices in overseeing worldwide emergencies. A proactive and arranged approach guarantees the coherence of sea exercises during testing times.

Grasp International Elements:

International contemplations altogether impact sea exchange. Organizations ought to put resources into understanding the international elements of key sea chokepoints, shipping lanes, and key areas. Remaining informed about international movements, political relations, and possible effects on shipping lanes is fundamental. Take part in discourse with applicable partners, including legislative bodies and international examiners, to explore the intricacies of global sea relations. Proactive commitment with international contemplations permits organizations to expect difficulties and settle on informed key choices.

Work together for Information Sharing and Interoperability:

In a time where information is a basic resource, organizations ought to effectively take part in drives for information sharing and interoperability. Team up with industry partners to lay out normal information guidelines, share significant data, and make interoperable frameworks. Shared information stages upgrade perceivability across the inventory network, work with smoother coordinated effort, and add to generally speaking industry effectiveness. Organizations that focus on information joint effort position themselves as vital supporters of an associated and smoothed out beach front trade environment.

Integrate Roundabout Economy Standards:

Economical and dependable strategic approaches include embracing roundabout economy standards. Organizations ought to plan to limit squander, reuse materials, and add to the circularity of assets inside the sea production network. Carrying out reusing programs, investigating the utilization of maintainable bundling, and taking on rehearses that diminish the natural effect of activities are key stages. Round economy standards line up with ecological maintainability objectives as well as add to long haul flexibility and dependable strategic approaches.

Take part in Local area Effort and Social Obligation:

Waterfront trade organizations are naturally associated with nearby networks. Participate in local area outreach programs, add to neighborhood advancement drives, and focus on friendly obligation. Lay out associations with nearby associations, support schooling and preparing programs, and put resources into projects that upgrade the prosperity of encompassing networks. Organizations that effectively take part in friendly obligation drives assemble positive connections, cultivate generosity, and add to the generally speaking financial advancement of the locales they work in.